SO YOU WANT TO BE A
PUPLIC SPEAKER

By the same author

*   *   *

SO YOU WANT TO BE A FREE-LANCE WRITER

SO YOU WANT TO BE A

PUBLIC

SPEAKER

By

GEORGE E. DIGGLE

MELKSHAM
COLIN VENTON

ISBN 0 85475 090 8

COPYRIGHT NOTICE

Set 11 on 12 point Intertype Baskerville
and printed in Great Britain
at the Press of the Publisher,
The Uffington Press,
Melksham, Wiltshire,
SN12 6LA, (U.K.).

LIST OF CONTENTS

FOR OLIVE

Her voice is ever soft, gentle and low;
an excellent thing in a woman.

Part I

UNACCUSTOMED AS I AM . . .

Chapter 1

WANTED! MORE GOOD SPEAKERS

The many occasions demanding speakers — organisations regularly requiring speakers — the purpose of public speaking — essentials of a good speech — you could succeed.

HAVE you ever stood up on your two feet and addressed an audience? Perhaps you did so at a wedding reception, where you were the best man. You listened to the father of the bride wishing health and happiness to the newly wed couple, and then to the bridegroom's somewhat hesitant and nervous reply. Then it was your turn! Trembling slightly at the knees, you bravely replied on behalf of the bridesmaids. You told the guests how, in your opinion, the bridesmaids were only second in charm and beauty to the bride herself — a rather neat turn of phrase, you privately thought. You told a family joke, and every one laughed heartily. You went on to read the congratulatory telegrams, carefully saving the wittiest until the last. You sat down amidst a storm of handclapping. Afterwards various guests sidled up to you, and told you how well you had acquitted yourself. In all honesty you had to agree with them. In fact they confirmed the opinion, forming in your mind, that you really did have a flair for public speaking. After the first few nervewracking moments you found, somewhat to your surprise, that you felt quite at home standing there, addressing an obviously interested and appreciative company. You feel, and the wedding guests have confirmed you in your feeling, that you undoubtedly have a talent, albeit an embryo talent, for public speaking. It would be a pity not to cultivate that talent,

7

and so let the community in general have the benefit.

But perhaps things did not work out so well as in the instance described above. You did manage, as best man, to get through your part without actually breaking down. But how you perspired, and stammered, and said "er", at least half a dozen times! You really did envy the father of the bride for the neat little speech he made. How easily and sincerely he spoke about the virtues and capabilities of the darling daughter he was losing—but to such a good fellow! How well he put over that anecdote about her charming ways as a four year old! How well he held the interest of the company! It must be grand to be able to stand up like that, and to have people hanging on to your words, to use an old cliché. How exciting it must be to have people waiting eagerly for the next gem of humour, or pearl of wisdom to fall from your lips! If he — who left school when he was fourteen years old — can make such an effective speech, why cannot you, whose formal education ended at 18, with 7 'O' levels and 2 'A' levels? Your voice is as strong as his, and certainly more cultured and refined. If he can, why not you?

Perhaps things worked out even worse than in the last instance. You are an enthusiastic member of the Women's Institute, priding yourself on your willingness to do everything possible to help to maintain the work. Then, one afternoon, your pride received a shock. The President asked you to do something you have never done before, namely, to second the vote of thanks to the speaker. In a state of near panic at the very thought of making a formal speech, however brief, you refused, very firmly and, you hope, courteously. The President saw that you meant what you said. She sighed, and asked a fellow member, who said "Yes" without any argument. Enviously you listened to the simple, sincere way in which this lady thanked the speaker. And this was her first attempt.

8

And the speaker that afternoon—you had known her all your life. You were educated at the same school. You noted how she obviously enjoyed talking to the assembly, and in answering the several questions that followed her address. If she could rise to all this, why cannot you? There was a time when she, like you at this present time, was unaccustomed to public speaking. If she could become accustomed, and enjoy it, as well as giving enjoyment to others, is there any good reason why you should not do so too?

It is probably true, as some assure us, that the great days of the public meeting are past. Our ancestors gathered, often in their thousands, for political and other meetings. Today we are content to remain by our own fireside, and listen to a party political broadcast on the little screen. The radio and the television bring the best in music, entertainment and public speaking right into our homes. But, in spite of this, people still attend concerts and music halls, for the real "live" performances. So, in spite of talks and discussions on the radio and on the television screen, people are still willing to leave their comfortable firesides if they feel there is something sufficiently worthwhile to justify their venturing forth. Another factor is the herd instinct. In spite of modern inventions people are still gregarious, and like to mix with their fellows. There is every indication that, in the foreseeable future, the good public speaker, male or female, will still be in demand. People may not gather in their thousands, as in Victorian and Edwardian times, but they still gather in their scores, and even in their hundreds, to listen to competent speakers.

Think of the many occasions when the public speaker is as much in demand as ever he was. To the weddings already mentioned, we may add other social occasions like coming of age parties, annual staff and club dinners, regimental and other reunions, presentations to retiring workers and others, the opening of fêtes, garden parties and bazaars, school prize and speech days, business and other conferences. The list is by no means exhaustive, and does not include, for instance, the many and constant religious occasions when a speaker is essential.

Think of the many organisations regularly requiring the services of speakers. To the Women's Institutes, already mentioned, we may add Townswomen's Guilds, Soroptimist Clubs, Rotary Clubs, the Inner Wheel, the Round Table, Parent-Teacher Associations, and others with which you may be acquainted. In business life the ability to address an audience effectively can be a great asset. The managing director, for instance, who is a persuasive speaker may well prevent friction which could lead to serious industrial trouble. From time to time executives are called upon to address their staffs, perhaps to explain some new policy, or to deliver a "pep talk". The political parties, especially at election times, both municipal and parliamentary, need able speakers.

Then there are the many and varied church gatherings on Sundays and weekdays, requiring both devotional and general speakers. On weekdays the Mothers' Union, the Women's Bright Hour, the Young Wives, the Men's Societies, the Guilds, the Fellowships, the Christian Endeavour Societies all need a constant supply of competent speakers. On Sundays every church needs its lay or ordained preacher. By no means does every weekday, or weeknight, meeting of a church organisation on church premises require a talk of a devotional nature. Talks on a wide variety of subjects, from how to bring up your children to the provision of guide dogs for the blind; from the work of a probation officer to experiences behind the Iron Curtain, are regularly delivered at meetings of church organisations on church premises. The demand and the scope for good speakers remains, and is likely to remain, very wide.

Having noted the part the public speaker can play in modern community life, we go on to ask whether you, the reader, can fit into the picture. We will presume that you are the possessor of a normal voice. That being so, at this early stage here are three basic questions for you to answer. An honest affirmative answer in each case indicates definite signs of promise.

1. Are you a reasonably good conversationalist? This implies that you are capable of explaining, or describing something—an experience or a personal or business problem—in which you are interested, to another person, or to a company or perhaps three or four people. Basically an audience is but an extension of this. If you can make yourself quite clear to a handful of people, there is good reason to hope that you could do the same to a larger company.

A good conversationalist goes straight to the point in his explanation or description. The rambler goes off down all kinds of sidetracks, and takes three or four times as long as it ought to take him to tell his tale. "You were asking about this new job of mine . . . yes, I'm settling in. The boss is a nice fellow, though I've heard that his wife's left him. But he's a nice fellow. And so long as I'm in my office by 9.30, that's all right. My colleague—chap who shares my office with me, comes to work in an old Jag. The boss' secretary's a nice girl. Lives near the park. By the way, have you noticed how lovely the rose gardens in the park look this year? Oh, yes! You were asking about my job! Do you know, Bill—that's the colleague, chap who shares my office, says he can get 90 out of that old Jag of his. But about my job—I can usually get away by 5 o'clock. But the traffic! It's about time the government did something about those hold-ups. It took me the best part of an hour to cover five miles last night . . . etc., etc.,

11

etc."

Sometimes ramblers like that actually get on to platforms and into pulpits! Oh, dear!

2. Are you willing to prepare thoroughly? That means things like pertinaceously hunting down relevant, but unusual and often elusive facts. It involves studying the background to your subject. It is to be willing to devote time and energy to thoroughly covering the ground, and more than the ground, that you propose to cover in your talk. It means forswearing the easygoing attitude of trusting to the inspiration of the moment when you stand up to speak. One of the greatest orators of this century, David Lloyd George, said that the surest way to inspiration is preparation. Conscientiousness may be one of the more pedestrian virtues, but it is an essential one for the speaker to practise.

3. Are you willing to be told your faults? If you resent criticism, however well meant and however tactfully put, you cannot hope to make progress. You are warned that honest criticism can hurt your pride. But without it you could go on for years making the same old mistakes irritating, or perhaps unwittingly amusing, your audiences with mannerisms that could have been corrected at the very beginning of your speaking career, if only you had had the grace to listen to an honest critic.

Novice speakers have been known to say to a friend, "Tell me, quite plainly, what you think about my speech. Don't pull any punches. Just give me the plain truth." What they hope to hear is something like this, "Excellent, old chap! Excellent! Not a word out of place! Not a word too many! You certainly gave it them straight! And witty too! I love your sense of humour! Yes, I thoroughly enjoyed your talk from beginning to end. Thank you, very much!"

12

But supposing the friend takes the speaker at his word and replies, "I thought you did well for a beginner. You'll have to watch the tone of your voice, and the pace of your delivery, and vary both. And, if I were you I think I'd cut out that little joke you told near the end. It did fall rather flat. It is rather a chestnut, you know. But you've nothing really to worry about. Keep it up. You're doing quite well."

A mild and moderate, and relevant criticism, one would think! Would you feel offended, misunderstood, and go away muttering something about damning a thing with faint praise, deeply disappointed because your friend did not laud your oratory to the skies? He would have been no true friend of yours if he had.

A man who is today a very acceptable speaker, much in demand for various kinds of meetings, dates the most significant growing point in his career to the time when, as a novice he received this broadside, "That monotonous voice of yours! If you don't do something about it, you'll degenerate into a prize sender of people to sleep! And what an enormous amount of ground you covered! Far too much! No one could possibly remember half of what you told us. And all those sidetracks you led us up, quite unnecessarily! You have a voice—like a fog horn at times! —and you don't yet know how to use it! You've plenty of material, but you don't know how to select and arrange it!"

Harsh? Rather hard on a beginner? Maybe, but the speaker will be wise to take the truth from the criticism, and forget the harshness. A sound maxim for all who would make progress in public speaking, or in any other form of activity, is—no criticism, no progress.

Were you able to say, "Yes" to those three basic questions? Then read on, for there is hope for you as a prospective public speaker.

One more point may engage your attention in all these

preliminary considerations. That is the question of motive. Just why do you want to be a public speaker? It would be more accurate to say motives, rather than motive, in the singular. Seldom do we engage in any activity from just one motive. In practice it is a question of which particular motive shall have priority. This truth certainly applies to public speaking. So let us be quite honest in assessing our mixed motives in this matter of speaking. Mixed motives are common to all speakers, whether they are saints or notorious sinners. The motive of self-display, "showing off", is found in all of us. The platform that exalts us above our fellows and affords us the satisfying sight of them respectfully receiving the pearls of wisdom that fall from our lips, provides the speaker with a first rate opportunity for displaying his ability.

A second motive is the quite natural desire to gain popularity, respect and maybe adulation through our platform efforts. There is also the "power" motive, the desire to influence people, to make them change their ways of thinking and acting. We might call these three the lower motives for wanting to become a public speaker. There is nothing to be ashamed about in owning up to them. They are part of our make-up as human beings, and as we shall see, they have their useful part to play. These lower motives are not the whole truth about the urge to speak in public. You feel you have a talent for addressing audiences. Life is only satisfactory if talents and capabilities are cultivated and used. A talent developed and put to good use is one form of self-fulfilment. To fail in this way is to impoverish ourselves, and to rob the community of the contribution we could have made. Here then, is an impeccable motive for stepping up on the platform. Man also has altruistic feelings, the desire to use his talents for the good of mankind. A talent for public speaking can be used to inform, broaden the mental outlook, influence for the better, and generally inspire to worthier ways of living. A talent to cultivate, and its use in the service of our fellows can be designated the higher motives for wanting to be a public speaker.

In the long run the greatest satisfaction comes to a speaker when the higher motives control the lower motives. These lower motives give us additional impetus in the pleasure that we feel in the respect and admiration we are accorded by our audiences. But let those lower motives take control, and we begin to "play to the gallery". The entertainment value of our talks increases, and so does their shallowness. We gain the applause of the unthinking, and the contempt of the thoughtful. We shun the unpopular view, which may be the right one, in favour of what "everybody" is thinking.

Mixed motives are common to us all. The great thing is frankly to recognise this, and then to observe the right priorities. This is done when the higher, and altruistic motives check and control the lower ones.

Wanted! More good speakers. We have noted the wide scope and demand for speakers in the modern world. We have noted some of the qualities that make a good speaker. He, or she, is a reasonably good conversationalist; capable of logical, orderly thought. The good speaker is thorough in preparation, and always willing to learn from critics, even if the criticism is sometimes given with an absence of tact and consideration for the speaker's feelings. A good speaker is aware of the mixed state of human motives, and takes care to get priorities right. All this, in addition to the possession of a reasonably good voice (which we will define in the next chapter). Given these qualities you have a foundation on which to build a satisfying career as a public speaker.

15

Chapter 2

MAKING THE BEST OF YOUR VOICE

Is speech training necessary? — give yourself a voice test —
use of the tape recorder — what to watch for — most faults
can be cured — use of the microphone.

Is a course of speech training essential for a potential
public speaker? The answer is "No", but we would qualify
that answer by adding that any public speaker would
benefit from such a course. If you have such an opportunity, take it. If, from time to time, an elocutionist, or teacher
of speech training is present in your audience, and is kind
enough to make some comments on your efforts, accept the
implied criticism with gratitude.

But the great majority of public speakers have had little
or no actual voice training. From books, (and there are
few things that books cannot help us to do better), and
from candid friends' comments, they have found their way
to some degree of effectiveness as speakers. While they
have been finding their way longsuffering audiences have
sometimes squirmed in their seats over the worst defects.
If your voice is harsh, blurred or squeaky, and you still
want to be a public speaker, then some training is absolutely necessary. If your voice is reasonably strong and clear,
you can become effective without a course in speech training, though you would almost certainly be more effective if
you did undertake such a course.

Have you access to a tape recorder? If so, you can
conduct your own voice test. Thanks to this invention it
is possible to hear yourself as others hear you, a revelation
that usually comes as a shock on the first hearing! For the

16

first time you may then realise the awful truth contained in the criticisms of your more candid hearers. Relentlessly the tape recorder shows up every fault in pronunciation, breathing and delivery. And we cannot accuse the tape of undue bias, hostility or jealousy! The defects are plainly recorded for the benefit of whoever has ears to want to hear. Having composed a talk on some subject that interests you, speak it into the microphone of the tape recorder in as near as possible the manner in which you would deliver it in public. Then play it back, and as the tape inexorably unwinds its so frankly revealing length, listen carefully for the major faults to which speakers are prone.

One such fault is monotony, a defect often accentuated by nervousness. It means saying everything in the one level tone of voice, without variation of either pitch of pace. No word is given greater emphasis than any other. The tape recorder may reveal that you read an exquisite poem by Shelley or Keats, or a passage in the matchless English of the Authorised Version, with no more expression than you would give to a page in the bus timetable! Few things are more calculated to make an audience lose interest, and to set them coughing, shuffling their feet, and looking at their watches, than a speaker who may have good material, but who drones on and on in a dreary monotone.

One way to combat this is to learn to emphasize the key words in sentences. The wide scope for this is often un-realised. A single short sentence of, say, six words, can be capable of six different emphasises. Suppose you were giving a talk on the inflationary tendencies of our time. The aim of your talk might be summed up in the words, "We can beat this menacing inflation." You have seven choices in the way you bring out that short sentence. You could deliver it with an equal emphasis on each word. How flat! Or you could take your choice from these six variations, according to your approach to the subject, and what has

17   2

preceded the vital sentence.

"WE can beat this menacing inflation!" the emphasis being on we, the people of Britain, who have weathered worse storms than this.

"We *CAN* beat this menacing inflation." You are trying to instil confidence.

"We can *BEAT* this menacing inflation." You are appealing to their fighting spirit.

"We can beat *THIS* menacing inflation." Perhaps you referred, earlier on in your talk, to the disastrous German monetary inflation of the 1920's. Even as they could beat that inflation, we British can beat this present one.

"We can beat this *MENACING* inflation." Your emphasis is upon the danger ahead, and the really dire results that could accrue.

"We can beat this menacing *INFLATION.*" Attention is focussed on the precise menace to be beaten.

Giving due emphasis to the key words, especially in the key sentences, adds life, as well as dramatic effect to your speech. It keeps the audience awake and alert, and therefore more receptive. A dull, heavy, monotonous style of delivery, all words being treated with more or less equal emphasis, is guaranteed to send an audience away deflated, and knowing little or no more than when they came. A lively, sometimes racy, style of speaking helps to get your facts across, and increases the demand for you as a speaker or lecturer.

The all-hearing tape will also reveal the presence or absence of a local accent. Unless you are so "broad" that people from other parts of Britain cannot follow you with ease, there is no occasion for undue concern. If you grew up in the north of England do not think it essential that you should cultivate a so-called "southern", "Oxford" or B.B.C. accent. At the same time you would be wise to eradicate any crude mispronunciations which could grate on the ears

18

of an educated audience. Your voice test on the tape recorder may indicate that no one has ever pointed out to you the difference in the correct pronunciation of the vowel sounds in words like "book" and "boot", "cook" and "cool", or "took" and "tool". In "book", "cook" and "took" the 'o' is the short form, as in "foot". Speakers have been known to go on for years, mispronouncing words like "book", "cook", "brook", "took", etc., provoking many a superior and private smile at their expense, just because no one had ever told them that we inconsistent English pronounce the sound "oo" in two different ways.

Watch also for the lazy way of speaking which neglects to bring out the consonants clearly. A piece of recently heard conversation ran like this.

"You remember Mr. Morra. . . ?"

"Mr. Morrow? Never heard of him."

"Of course you have. He knows you, does Mr. Morra . . . ."

Light dawns! "Oh, you mean Mr. Mottram! Of course I know him!"

In some parts of the country the letter 't' tends to be left out, and we hear of "a bi' o' bu'er, and a piece o' mea' pa'y." Watch the consonants, and give them their due place, if you wish to be heard clearly.

Pronunciation of the letter 'r' is another pitfall for some speakers. Listen carefully to that recording. Do you say, "I sawr him"? Words ending in "aw" do not need an 'r' sound. Chop them off short.

Then there is the matter of aspirates—your dealings with the letter 'h'. Are you quite at home with this letter, knowing just when to omit its sound, as well as to give it is rightful place? There are less than a dozen words in the English language where the 'h' at the beginning is silent— hour, heir, heiress, honest, honesty, honestly, honour, honourable, and honourably. All the rest of those hundreds

19

of words in the dictionary beginning with 'h' require your attention, if you wish to make a favourable impression on the average audience. Nor should you forget the 'h' in words like "what", "why", "when" and "where".

If you find yourself dropping the 'h' from time to time at the beginning of words that require it, make up some sentences like this, and practise saying them aloud.

"Help Albert Herbert Handsworth and Helen Amy Eccles' Uncle Henry, and Horace Edward Humbert to enjoy a happy evening out on Hampstead Heath."

To go over that kind of sentence, fairly quickly, getting every 'h' in its right place will help you to overcome any weakness in that direction.

The kind of voice to cultivate is a clear and carrying one, rather than a particularly loud one. The difference between clarity and inaudibility often lies in the way a speaker uses his consonants—or, as we have seen, does not use them. A good vowel sound, with a clear beginning and ending, is the key to being heard by every one with normal hearing. To make the best use of your voice stand up straight, and speak from the lungs, rather than from the throat. Good speakers never suffer from that affliction known as clergyman's sore throat. To speak from the lungs, it is necessary to fill the lungs with air, and to keep on filling them as required as your talk proceeds. Recognise that your voice has two registers, an upper and a lower one, and use them both. Use the lower register for the more serious parts of your speech, and the upper one for the lighter parts. Remember to keep up your voice at the end of your sentences, or the audience may lose your meaning.

This hint also applies to a single matter like announcing the number of a hymn in a church service. The novice (and sometimes the experienced person who ought to know better), will announce, "Number seven hundred and sixty

20

five," with a distinct dropping of the voice on the last figure which sets the congregation looking at one another enquiringly about the exact number they are supposed to turn up. Make it "Seven hundred and sixty FIVE", with a distinct emphasis and a slight raising of the voice on the "five".

In order to obtain a dramatic effect some speakers resort to dropping their voices almost to a whisper. You can only get away with this if you take special care to speak very clearly indeed. Otherwise the effect of your intended dramatic climax is entirely spoiled. In any case it is doubtful whether the slightly deaf in the audience will be able to hear a very softly spoken passage. You are on safer ground if you raise your voice, and slow down the pace for your dramatic climax.

If you happen to be speaking in a small hall, do not fall into the error of thinking that an ordinary conversational voice is enough. To enable all the people to hear comfortably a little more volume is necessary than if you were talking to just one or two people by your fireside. The amount of extra volume may not be much, but it is that little much which makes all the difference between some people hearing without straining, or having to strain, and then missing perhaps vital passages.

Whatever the size of the hall, speak to the people on the back row. You can then be sure that the people on the other rows will also hear in comfort. If you speak to the company in general, and not to any particular row, you run the risk of being inaudible in the back part of the hall. In the opening part of your speech, watch those people at the back. Do they look strained, or does the expression on their faces say, "There's no difficulty in hearing him (her)."?

In many halls, even medium sized ones, a microphone may be available. If you are in any doubt at all about making yourself heard, avail yourself of its use. If you have never used a microphone before, there is no occasion to be scared of it! After a little experiment you will be so glad it was there to save any strain on your voice, and to enable everyone in the largest hall to follow you without difficulty. There are certain disadvantages to the use of the microphone. If you are one of those speakers who like to take a turn up and down the platform now and again, the microphone can cramp your style. You must stay near to the microphone. At a distance of 1 ft. from the instrument you can talk in a quiet, restrained tone, as if you were talking to just one person in your own home. At a distance of 3-4 ft. you can speak in an ordinary voice, and be heard comfortably in the largest hall. Whatever you do, don't shout, for the sake of the ear drums of the audience, as well as for the favour you will lose in so doing. If the instrument crackles and booms, some mechanical fault may be responsible, but the fault is much more likely to be yours. You are too near and too loud. The microphone definitely discourages the full use of the voice. See that the microphone is set at the right height, and when you are talking, look at the audience, not at the microphone.

How can you make the best use of the voice with which nature has endowed you? In a nutshell :

Take advantage of any opportunity of speech training that comes your way.

Beware of Enemy No. 1—monotony of delivery. Defeat it by varying tone, pitch and pace, and by giving the key words their due emphasis.

Eradicate crudities, either of local accent, or of pronunciation.

Beware of the laziness that neglects to bring out the sound of the consonants.

Speak from the chest, not from the throat, by keeping the lungs well filled.

22

Use the upper and the lower registers of the voice.

Speak to the people on the back row.

Accept, with thankfulness, the two modern inventions—the tape recorder and the microphone—and exploit their possibilities to the full.

It is a good thing to do all you can to find out your vocal faults and weaknesses at the very beginning of your speaking career, before they become more and more deeply ingrained, and therefore so much the harder to eradicate. Habits are as important in the matter of public speaking as in any other sphere of life. The establishment of good habits from the very beginning, and the rooting out of bad ones before they have time to establish themselves still further, and mar your speaking career, is therefore of paramount importance. One good habit to establish is to listen humbly and respectfully to your critics, whether the mechanical kind or the candid, knowledgeable human kind.

Chapter 3

NERVOUSNESS—THE MAJOR OBSTACLE

Universal problem — symptoms — its purpose — irrational
fears — no short cuts — when you face the audience —
importance of thorough preparation — when you "dry up" —
practice makes perfect.

"OH, I could never stand up, and make a speech! I'd be
much too nervous! I'm sure I'd break down before I'd
said half a dozen words! And what a fool I'd look then,
wouldn't I?"

A great many people who once thought and spoke like
that have developed into capable, efficient public speakers.
Although nervousness, sometimes called stage fright, or just
"nerves" is the major obstacle to success in public speaking,
it can be overcome. Thousands of sought-after speakers can
testify to that. The first thing to note about this problem
is that it is a universal one among would-be speakers. You
are not the exception, and if so many others have overcome
there is no good reason why you should not likewise succeed. The symptoms of nervousness are many. The heart
pounds away in an almost alarming manner. The knees
tremble, butterflies seem to be flying around inside the
stomach. There may be a confusion, or a drying up, of
thought. Speech may be slow, hesitant, even stammering;
or the words may come pouring out in a manner suggesting
that your greatest desire is to get through your speech in
record time. Underlying all this is a general lack of confidence in your ability to hold the favourable attention of the
audience for the duration of the speech.

Experienced speakers confess to feelings of nervous tension before addressing a meeting. But they go on to say

that this feeling invariably leaves them when they are actually on their feet, facing the audience. Nervousness is, in fact, a perfectly natural phenomenon. It is Nature's way of preparing us for a challenging situation. The brain has sent a message to your adrenal glands, situated above the kidneys. These pour an infinitesimal amount of the drug adrenalin into your blood stream. The heart is provoked into increased activity—hence that pounding sensation. This makes more blood available for any muscular task. The muscles involved in breathing are stimulated to provide additional oxygen for the work to be performed. The adrenalin also causes sugar to be released, providing extra energy. All this happens automatically, without any conscious willing on your part, beyond the knowledge of an impending challenge. There is, therefore, nothing whatever to be ashamed about in feeling nervous. Nature is at work, doing her share by providing the necessary energy for you to make a successful speech. The only shame could be in your shirking, rather than responding to, the challenge. As thousands can testify, there are ways and means of controlling this natural increase of nervous energy, so that it is used for its proper purpose. Like other forms of power, controlled it is a blessing, uncontrolled it is a menace.

Much of the apprehension concerning nervousness lies in a lack of self-confidence, grounded in irrational fear. Take this point well to heart — there is much that is irrational, unreasonable, in the beginner's attitude to nervousness. There is fear of breaking down, fear of making a fool of oneself, fear of failure to communicate whatever it is we are trying to communicate, fear of the audience and its response. We are so anxious to be a great success, and to be held in high regard—again, something which is quite natural.

Let us take a long, cool look at these several fears. Let us take the fear of breaking down. How many times

25

have you seen, or even heard of, a speaker actually breaking down, and having to sit down in great confusion and distress, in the middle of his speech? Once? Twice? Or never? It is comforting to face the fact that a breakdown is a very rare occurrence indeed.

The fear of failing to communicate your message, and so of feeling foolish, is a more real one. Effective ways to get the message across will be described later in this book. What about fear of the audience? Occasionally this may be well founded. In a political meeting you could well find yourself facing a hostile, unsympathetic audience, people all too ready to show their contempt for you, and for what you stand. But this kind of audience attitude is the exception, rather than the rule. An audience composed almost entirely of people who have known you for years, perhaps all your life, can worry a beginner. The prevalent attitude may be one of natural curiosity. They are wondering what kind of a job the local lad is going to make of it! The curiosity, in some cases, may be mingled with a little jealousy. They may be realising that you are doing something they haven't the nerve to do, even if they had the ability! The natural curiosity may be mingled with a spirit of slightly hostile criticism. There is nothing at all new in this. Nearly two thousand years ago it was observed that a prophet is not without honour save in his home town! It's all part of the challenge!

In the vast majority of instances you do not need to worry at all about the attitude of your audience. If they know that you are a beginner they will be sympathetic, and may not expect too much from you. They will be ready to make allowance for your novice state. They will wish you well. They are with you—at the beginning of your talk, at any rate. How to keep them with you right to the end will be explained in due course.

In facing up to the facts that your fears may be liars,

you have taken one step towards the control of that natural feeling of nervous tension, as body and mind key themselves up to face the task before them.

Beware of any so-called short cuts to the overcoming of nervous tension. Knowing ones may advise you to take a nip, or several nips if necessary, of something alcoholic before mounting the platform. "You'll forget all about your nerves, you won't know you have any then, old man!" they will say. They may go on to recount instances of brilliant and spellbinding speeches made by ordinarily shy, retiring people, under the influence of a nip or two. It is true that alcohol makes you feel relaxed—a great asset for a speaker. Alcohol's immediate effect is one of euphoria —a sense of wellbeing, and of confidence in yourself. What more could a nervous speaker desire? But this is only one side of the coin. Why do sensible, responsible motorists refrain from drinking before or during driving? While they feel they are driving so much better, the actual fact is that their re-actions are dangerously slowed down and their judgment blurred. The same natural law applies to public speaking. The amount of alcohol necessary to produce the desired effect of being on top the world may be bought at the price of blurred delivery, and a speech that may be confused, and even nonsensical. Alcohol clouds the judgment of the speaker, as well as that of the car driver. When question time comes you will need a clear head, if you are to acquit yourself well. Alcohol is as much the enemy of the public speaker as it is of the car driver. Stick to water! It makes no false promises, and just provides that necessary lubrication your throat may need from time to time.

Experienced speakers sometimes offer us hints on their own particular technique of overcoming nervousness. In the early years of the present century a certain Duke explained his method to young Winston Churchill, who

27

sat beside him on the platform of the Free Trade Hall, Manchester. "Are you nervous, Winston?" the Duke enquired. "Yes," was the frank reply. "I used to be," said the Duke, and went on to tell how he had overcome his disability. He told how, that when he mounted a platform, it was his custom to take a good look at the audience, before he sat down. Then he would say to himself, "I never saw such a lot of d . . . . fools in my life." After this, he claimed that he felt a lot better. While we do not commend the Duke's superior and condescending, in fact frankly insulting, attitude in its entirety, there is a golden grain of commonsense in his uncomplimentary summing up of his audience. In his own peculiar way the Duke reminded himself that he was not inferior to, but at least the equal of the people he had come to address. When you appear on the platform, look around your audience by all means, but in a realistic rather than in a snobbish, insulting way. It is a quite legitimate, as well as a practical move on your part, to ask yourself how many of them have the nerve, or the ability, to take your place up there on the platform. That puts you, at least, on a level with them, and dismisses that irrational feeling of inferiority. You have taken one more step towards the full control of that nervous energy welling up within you, enabling you to accomplish what you came to do.

The great moment now approaches. The chairman has told the audience something about your background and accomplishments, and shows signs of drawing to an end of his (we hope) brief remarks. As the end of this introduction approaches it is a good plan to take in half a dozen deep breathes. This not only has a steadying effect on the nerves, but also increases the amount of energy—giving oxygen in your blood. The chairman announces your name. You stand up smartly, and face the audience squarely. If you cannot produce a charming smile, at least do your

NERVOUSNESS — THE MAJOR OBSTACLE

best to look pleasant. Take your stance firmly, but at ease, on your two feet. If one leg shows an inclination to twine around the other, pull it back at once. Resist any temptation to loll, or to seek support by leaning on the table, (which is usually too low for the purpose, anyway), or on the reading desk—if one is provided. Let your two legs assume full responsibility for supporting you in a vertical position. They are quite adequate for the job, unless you are a partial cripple, or afflicted in some way by rheumatism, arthritis, sciatica, or other distressing complaint. Then, before you speak, make quite sure that your lungs are well filled with air. Having to take a breath in the middle of your very first sentence will not help to create that desirable favourable impression upon your hearers. At this stage in the proceedings the great thing is to act confidently, even if you do not feel confident. Refuse to be ruled by your feelings. This is not so difficult as it sounds. How often, when the clock says, "Get out of bed", you feel like turning over and enjoying another hour of sleep! But you set aside your feelings, and rise to begin another day's work. If you are not ruled by your feelings in the bedroom, why should you be on the platform? Act confidently, and you begin to feel confident.

But all this preliminary work will have been in vain if you have not been thorough in the preparation of the contents of your speech. The following questions will indicate just how thorough you have been in your preparation. Has your research been limited strictly to the amount of ground you propose to cover in your address, or have you covered much more ground than is strictly necessary? The fact that your study of your subject took you far beyond the limits of your talk will, in itself, generate confidence that you will be equal to the demands for further information your questioners may make.

Have you checked, and if necessary, re-checked your

facts and figures, and can you state your authority for quoting them?

Are you quite satisfied that the arguments you put forward in support of your proposition are really sound? Have you imagined yourself in the place of an objector, and tried to see your proposals from his angle?

Have you gone to much trouble to make your explanations crystal clear, free from all ambiguity, so that no person of normal intelligence could mistake your meaning? This pre-supposes that you are not in the least hazy in your own mind about what you propose to tell your hearers, and about precisely what you are asking them to believe or do.

Did you keep the type of audience awaiting you in mind as you prepared your talk? Instead of putting everything you know about the subject in your address, did you consciously make a selection of the facts and arguments most likely to appeal to that particular audience?

Do you feel a really deep interest in your subject? If your subject really grips you, then you will tend to forget your fears. If your subject does not really grip you, there is little prospect of it gripping your audience. For that reason it is usually wise to refuse an invitation to speak on some subject in which your interest is slight. If you cannot interest yourself deeply in a subject, you can hardly expect to interest your audience in the same way. Sincerity and enthusiasm in a speaker have a way of communicating themselves to his hearers.

Have you brought well compiled notes with you on to the platform? This means notes that can be referred to quickly and easily in the event of an interruption, or a request for recapitulation. It means notes set out in a clear and orderly manner, so that the speaker follows them without difficulty, and the necessity to make pauses in his speech while he consults them. How to compile such notes will be fully explained in a later chapter.

If you can answer "Yes" to all these questions you can face your hearers with confidence. A wider knowledge of your subject is strictly necessary for that talk; facts and figures verified; arguments tested for soundness; crystal clear explanations; facts selected and slanted towards that particular audience; the speaker's deep and sincere interest in his subject; properly compiled notes — these are the marks of good preparation.

Occasionally, in spite of adequate preparations, your mind may suddenly become blank in the middle of your talk. Do not panic! There is nothing to be worried about in this kind of occasional lapse. Remember that you are under a certain amount of strain, and that even experienced speakers confess to an occasional temporary "drying up" of their mental processes. You are in no way exceptional if you find that, from time to time, your brain "stalls". When thought ceases, pause for a moment. Blow your nose, or clear your throat, and take a drink of water. You will find that the brief rest is sufficient. The brain begins to function again, and thoughts begin to flow. One cause of such lapses is that your mind has become slightly distracted from the subject. In that case the remedy is obvious. Keep a firmer grip on your thoughts.

The trite old saying that practice makes perfect is as true of public speaking as of any other subject. There is nothing like regular and constant speaking to make a speaker! With this in mind take every possible opportunity that offers of getting on your feet in public and talking. If you are a member of an audience at a public meeting, make yourself get on your feet when question time comes. Ask a question—any question, so long as it is a sensible one, even if you know the answer! Or you can ask the speaker to elaborate on some point upon which you are not quite clear. Anything to get you on your feet in public,

31

thinking and talking. If a debate is in progress, make yourself join in, if possible with some fact or argument not already brought out, when the floor is declared open to all. Offer your services to propose, or to second, a vote of thanks, and win the gratitude of the secretary, who is sometimes hard pressed to find volunteers for this necessary courtesy. Every time you perform some little act of this kind you win another victory over the major enemy, and you take another step forward feeling thoroughly at home on a platform, addressing a large audience. Constant practice, secure in the knowledge that you are well prepared, is the royal road to the overcoming of nervousness, that major obstacle to effective public speaking. Take that road, and perhaps surprisingly soon you'll be asking almost incredulously, "Did I ever really say I could never stand up, and make a speech, because I'd be too nervous?"

Part II

PREPARATION

Chapter 4

STUDY YOUR AUDIENCE

What is the object of your speech? — study potential audience
with that in mind — types of people likely to be present —
why have they come? — what approach is most likely to
appeal to them?

How long did it take to prepare your lunch? Let us assume that you enjoyed a simple meal of roast lamb,
potatoes, and cabbage, followed by apple pie and custard.
The vegetables had to be prepared and cooked, the meat
roasted, the apples peeled and cored, the pastry made and
the resulting pie cooked. The making of the gravy and the
custard, and the setting of the table completed the process.
A couple of hours, or so, of preparation and you sat down
to a simple, but appetising meal.

But that is only the end of the full story of the
preparation of your lunch. A couple of hours, or so, to
prepare? How long did it take to grow the potatoes and
the cabbage? How long to raise the sheep? How long to
grow the corn to make the flour for the pie crust? Months,
and years, of preparation lie behind the preparation of a
simple meal. It is like that, too, with the preparation of
the mental meal you offer your hearers when you deliver a
speech.

You have a talk to prepare. You sit down, and work
really hard for two or three hours. If you are a beginner,
and even if you are a speaker of some experience, you
write out in full what you propose to say. You revise,
re-arrange your points, you polish the sentences and
phrases until you feel you have something of a sufficiently
high standard to offer to your prospective audience. "It

33   3

took me three hours of hard work to prepare that talk," you tell your friends.

In actual fact you began your preparation of that talk years ago, when you learned to read and write. Your preparation continued down the years as you read widely, absorbed information from the radio and television, mixed with people, and generally absorbed the knowledge and experience of life that lie behind the speech you are currently preparing. Your cultural life, the people you have lived with and worked with, and the way life has treated you, have all combined to prepare you to make the talk on which you are now engaged. The efforts you are making today to keep abreast of the times are preparing you for the speeches you will be making in the months and years ahead. Preparation should be going on all the time, and it comes to a head when you actually get down to the details of your next speech.

We will assume that your studies, and your experience of life, entitle you to accept an invitation to speak at some gathering. Having provided yourself with a good supply of paper and ballpoint pens, you seat yourself at a table or desk to begin what is, in reality, the last stage of preparation. The first thing, the very first thing, to be perfectly clear about in your mind is just what you are trying to do. Exactly what do you hope to achieve by giving this talk? Do you wish to convey information, to broaden your hearers' outlook on some aspect of life? This, in itself, is a good thing, for many people would enjoy life much more if their general outlook on what the world has to offer was not so restricted. Do you wish to change their way of thinking about your subject, as a prelude to a change in behaviour? Behind actions lie thoughts, and if you can change the thought you change the action. Just what do you aim to accomplish? Get that quite clear in your mind, and write it down at the head of your paper, as a reminder

34

if needed. Having your aim quite clear in your mind, your next step is to consider that aim in relation to the particular audience you have been invited to address.

The actual form of your address will depend, in large measure, upon the type of audience to whom you will deliver it. If the meeting is a local one this point will present no difficulty. If the audience will be made up of people who are strangers to you, ask the secretary, or whoever invited you, just what kind of people you are expected to address. Try to get a mental picture of your audience, and keep that picture in the forefront of your mind as you prepare. If you are in any doubt about the composition of the audience, ask the secretary, or the person who issued the invitation, questions like these.

About how many people can be expected to attend?

Will they be of one sex, or mixed?

What age group, if any, will predominate; or will there be a cross section of ages from adolescents to senior citizens?

Will children be present in any numbers?

Tactfully enquire about the intelligence level. Would they be willing to think, or would they be just bored if you made demands on their mental equipment?

What knowledge, if any, of your subject can you reasonably assume?

What of their social status? Council estate? Suburban? County? Or a mixture of all three?

All these factors need to be taken into account as you proceed with your preparation. Overlook them, and you prepare an address which may reflect your own good and mature tastes, but not their's. You may have prepared an excellent, informative, thought-provoking address, but if you have allowed yourself and your tastes to obtrude unduly, and have overlooked the viewpoints of the majority of the audience, you will be ineffective.

Suppose you are invited to talk to a group mixed in

35

age, sex, intelligence and background. Your best plan then is to try to include something for everybody. Try to talk about one or other of our basic human instincts and needs, and you find you have a universal appeal. If you try to tell them how to meet some practical need, you will find that they listen readily. Notice the rapt attention given to the police officer, as he tells how to protect your house, or other property, from the unwelcome attentions of the burglar; or to the fire officer, as he tells what to do in case of a conflagration in your home; or to the lecturer on hygiene as he explains how to prevent yourself from becoming a victim to food poisoning. The success of these speakers is due, not only to the homely, friendly way in which they present their facts, but also to their appeal to the instinct of self-preservation implanted in every one of us.

A speaker dealing with the subject of pollution can appeal, not only to the instinct of self-preservation, but also to that of pugnacity, as he shows what each one of us can do to fight this menace to our planet. The wise speaker, appealing to man's fighting spirit, will as far as possible attack problems rather than actual personalities. By doing so he will keep on the right side of the laws of slander. If he refers to people he will usually do so in general, rather than in specific terms. Denounce a party, if you must, but be very careful about denouncing specific leaders or members of the party.

In every one of us, too, there is a tender instinct. You can appeal to this by references to babies, pets and helpless creatures generally. Appeal to basic human instincts, and show how practical needs can be met, and you need not fear that you will be unable to interest the average audience. People are always interested in people. It is a good thing to refer to the sayings and doings of actual people, by way of illustration of the ideas you are trying to put across. But select some one whose name is familiar to that audience.

36

An audience of senior citizens, for example would be more responsive to a reference to Lloyd George, Horatio Bottomley or Pearl White, than would an audience whose average age was under 40. If you were addressing a meeting of the Mothers' Union, a reference to the life or sayings of Mary Sumner, the founder of that movement, would be well received. But in a Young Wives' meeting the same reference might well fall flat, whereas a quotation from the writings of Marj Proops would probably provoke smiles of agreement all round.

Another point to be borne in mind as you begin your preparation is the probable mood of the audience. How far will they be with you from the beginning? Are you likely to face a hard task in bringing them round to your point of view? If you feel that they will be difficult to convince, imagine yourself discussing the subject with a typical objector. Think of all the awkward questions he would be likely to raise. Do not shirk them, but try to answer the objections quite honestly in your own mind. This, in itself, will influence the general trend of the address you are preparing.

Do not let your appeal be directed solely to the intellect. You may marshall your arguments, and present them in a masterly manner, yet fail to win the audience to your viewpoint. Your sound, solid, closely reasoned speech may just weary them, instead of sending them away full of enthusiasm and determination to do what you wanted them to do. In short, you must appeal to the emotions, as well as to the intellect. Man is a creature of feeling, as well as of thinking. A great deal of nonsense is talked about appealing to the emotions. Our emotions are just as genuine a part of our make-up as are our minds. Just because some unscrupulous orators have exploited the emotions of simple people there is no cause for us to neglect this side of our nature. In fact no really satisfying speech does neglect the emotions of the audience.

Read some of the stirring speeches made over the radio by Winston Churchill, in the darkest days of the 2nd World War. Note the way in which he presents hard facts. There was no room for sloppy sentimentality there! Yet listeners were deeply stirred by the dogged, no-surrender spirit, and the national morale was accordingly strengthened.

There is food for thought in Aldous Huxley's brief description of a man speaking at Tower Hill, on the theme of peace. "He spoke well—the right mixture of arguments, jokes, emotional appeal." The emotions, like anger, fear and pity, are the great driving forces of life. Do not be afraid to appeal to them—but let the appeal be based on indisputable facts. Note, too, the words "the right mixture". The right proportions of argument and emotional appeal vary from audience to audience. Growing experience will help you to judge "the right mixture" for that particular audience. Some hold the view that women are creatures of emotion, while men look for hard facts and watertight arguments before they can be convinced. There may be a modicum of truth in this, but a speaker who took that idea too seriously would be in for a some unpleasant shocks. Your study of your audience will take into account their emotional potential, as well as their intelligence.

When you have decided just what you hope to accomplish by making your speech, preparation begins in the study of the audience to whom you will address your talk. Find out all you can about them — their sex, cultural background, age group or groups — anything that will guide you in the selection of suitable material, and the way you will present it to them. This is an absolute essential preliminary if you wish to be effective. Another golden rule is to try to put yourself in their place, in an attempt to get into their minds and see things from their outlook. You

38

will then be in a position to estimate, more or less accurately, the kind of material and presentation that will appeal to them, intellectually and emotionally. Never assume that what interests you very deeply will necessarily make the same profound appeal to them.

Study your audience, as thoroughly as possible, and you have taken the first step in adequate preparation to address them effectively.

Chapter 5

YOUR MATERIAL

Write down what you know — other sources — select relevant
facts — assemble in logical order — use of examples and
quotations.

You are quite clear in your own mind about the precise
object of your speech. You have found out all you can
about the type of audience you can expect. With these
two vital points of information in mind you can proceed
to the next step in the preparation of the talk—the collecting, assembling and arranging of suitable material.

Begin by writing down everything you can think of that
may be relevant to your theme. A day or two later, read
over these rough notes, and strike out everything that, on
second thoughts and after due reflection, you feel to be not
strictly relevant. This will prevent you, when the time
comes to deliver the speech, from leading your hearers
down all kinds of interesting, but quite unnecessary sidetracks.

Keep a special little notebook in your pocket or handbag.
Write down, at once, any additional points as and when
they occur to you. Do not trust too much to your memory.
That brilliant thought may prove most exasperatingly
elusive when you try to recall it. Capture it, once and for
all, by writing it down at the time.

Thoughts that bubble up in your own mind, rather than
are taken from books, are especially valuable. They can
give local colour, and a personal slant that will give a
distinctive flavour to the resulting talk.

Side by side with this you will be undertaking the necessary research into your subject. This will vary according to

the nature of your theme. It may involve interviewing, or writing letters to knowledgeable people and organisations. It could involve inspecting old Minute Books, old newspapers, reports and records. You may need to consult various works of reference to be found in the local reference library. There you will find standard works of reference covering a wide variety of subjects, like the "Daily Mail Yearbook," and "Whittaker's Almanack," directories of towns and trades. If your talk is to be about local history, the Victoria County Histories and Arthur Mee's series of County Books will help you. If you are to talk on some aspect of literature or music, the Oxford Companions to those subjects may fill in some gaps in your background knowledge. The Oxford Books of verse and quotations are two other useful compilations. If your talk is about some famous person or persons no longer with us, the multi-volumed Dictionary of National Biography, and "Who was Who," are helpful. If you are to speak about some living person, "Who's Who" will be of use. In addition to all these the standard encyclopaedias and dictionaries will also be found to hand on the shelves of any reference library. If, in spite of this formidable array of knowledge you still cannot find the facts you need, the librarian will be pleased to help you. Try to track down little known facts. These will add appreciably to the interest of your talk. At the same time note the source of your information. This will be of help if you are challenged on its accuracy. It is a good idea to note the sources of all the information you collect, and to be ready to quote them as your authorities, if necessary, in question time. You are also advised, if at all possible, to check on the astonishing information imparted to you by the oldest inhabitant before passing it on to an audience one of whose members may be in a position to expose it as nonsense.

Having now collected a mass of information, your next

task is to make a selection of those key points most likely to interest your hearers. Beginners sometimes make the mistake of trying to include everything they know about a subject. Instead of trying to cram everything into one talk, it is far better to take one aspect, and to deal thoroughly with that. At the same time you should know much more about a subject than you divulge in one talk. You will appreciate the relevance of this at question time, when other angles and aspects are discussed. It is a good thing to have plenty of information in reserve, just in case people want to know more than you have been able to tell them in your allotted time.

One talk, one aspect of a subject, is a good rule, and saves you from ending up resembling an incompetent salesman who is trying to sell six things at once! Having decided on your angle on your theme, select and assemble such material as will make a coherent story. Concrete examples of what you are talking about give colour and human feeling to the address. Well chosen, relevant anecdotes add greatly to the interest and effect. Apt quotations are another help. But keep them short, and be quite sure to quote accurately, and to ascribe the words to the person who actually said them. Do not assure an audience that, "They say that money is the root of all evil," when the actual wording was "The love of money"—a totally different thing. If you plan to declaim, with dramatic effect, "Here I stand, I can do no other," ascribe the words to Martin Luther, and not to St. Paul, as one speaker did, thereby losing himself the respect of the more intelligent part of his audience. Be sparing in the number of quotations you make, and do not select the more hackneyed ones. Long quotations, no doubt very profound, hold up the progress of the talk, and tend to lose your audience interest. Latin tags and foreign expressions are best left out. They suggest a showing off of superior knowledge and education on your part, and in any case, some of the audience will not understand them.

Let us see how all this works out in practice, by taking a specific subject, and then building up a talk about it. Local history is a popular subject, especially with older people, and is in demand at all kinds of meetings. Rotary Clubs, Townswomen's Guilds, Women's Institute, Workers' Educational Association, evening classes, as well as a variety of church meetings will all eagerly lap up a well constructed talk on local history. Residents of longstanding will revel in old times recalled, and new residents will welcome information about the place they now live in.

First decide on the angle from which you will treat your subject. You could give your hearers a potted version of the story of your town, which may go back many centuries. This would interest the new residents, but the older ones have probably heard all that before. By giving a general outline of your town's history you may well be telling the majority of your hearers what they already know. It might be more rewarding to pick out a particular period in your town's history, perhaps the Victorian, and enlarge on the state of affairs at that time, rather than by trying to cover perhaps a thousand years. Another good idea is to pick out one particular year, say forty, fifty or sixty years ago, and describe life in your town as it was then. Or you could select some momentous year, like 1914, or 1939, for this kind of treatment. Alternatively, according to the composition of your audience, you could deal with some particular side of life in the town down the years. The industrial development, or transport, or the sporting and entertainment sides of local life over the years are other possibilities. In church meetings the religious developments in the town are an obvious choice, with greatest emphasis on the denomination concerned, but not to the total exclusion of others.

Whatever angle you take, heed well the words of the

43

great social historian, G. M. Trevelyan, "The appeal of history is imaginative . . . to behold our ancestors as they really were, going about their daily business, and their daily pleasure." In other words, keep the human element well to the fore! Take that as your guide line, and when you have had your say, your hearers will sit and talk and talk, and not want to go home! This rule still applies even if you are addressing a serious-minded body of people like the local historical society, or a meeting of the Workers' Educational Association. Even then you should be sparing in the amount of extracts you may read from medieval documents or from the Town Council Minutes. Tell them something about the men and women behind the documents.

The sources of your information include old residents, old local and county directories, any local histories and the back files of the local newspaper. The last-named can often be inspected at the offices of the newspaper concerned. If yours is a progressive town you may find that you are saved from the labour of turning over the dusty, yellowing, brittle pages of the old newspapers in your search for information. Many libraries have arranged for the back numbers of the local paper to be photographed—one whole year's issues on one small roll of film. You insert this roll into the micro-film reader, and the wording is projected on to a small screen, something like a television screen. Turn a small knob, and the magnified pages pass before your eyes at will.

You have been invited to address a meeting composed largely of senior citizens. After due consideration you decide that you will talk about their, and your, town as it was in that year of destiny, 1914, when many of your hearers were young. Your talk could be modelled on the popular radio "Scrapbook" programmes, giving glimpses of many sides of life in your town in that momentous year. Material for such a talk is available in the pages of the local newspaper for that year. From that source you can build up an authentic picture of town life of the period. Your talk will include references to the leading personalities in the municipal, industrial, church, and sporting life of the day.

You could take your hearers for an imaginary stroll round their town as it was in 1914, reminding them of various buildings no longer with us, and of green fields or woods now covered over with houses.

The prowess of the local football team, what was show at the cinemas, and what was being played at the theatre will be of interest to your audience.

The church life of the town, referring to any available statistics of attendances, and the number of Sunday School scholars, for comparative purposes, together with a reference to any famous preacher who visited the town is another item to be included.

The men present might like to be reminded of the rates of pay, and the working conditions, current in local industry at the time. The ladies will be interested to compare the prices of food and clothing then with those of the present day.

What was the crime situation? Was any notable crime committed in your town that year? How many "drunks" were prosecuted? Were there any areas of slum property, now cleared away? What of educational facilities, and of the cultural life generally? How did matters of health—infant mortality and disease, compare with today?

Since 1914 saw the outbreak of the 1st World War, just how much, or how little was life in the town affected during the early months of the conflict? Were any of the young men of the town members of the British Expeditionary Force—the Old Contemptibles—and did some distinguish themselves for gallantry, perhaps in the retreat from Mons?

Look for quaint, or unusual, sidelights on life in the town. Quote any complimentary or rude remarks and opinions about the town as it was then. A northern manufacturing town was, for instance, summed up at that time as "Renowned for good soap and bad smells."

A good way of rounding off your address would be to invite hearers to consider just how much real progress had been made in the general life and condition of the town since those early 20th century days. To guide them in their discussion you could remind them that progress can be judged by material, moral, intellectual and artistic standards, and that the world has seldom progressed in all these ways at the same time.

Your talk finished, the meeting is thrown open for questions, comments and discussions. A fierce argument arises between two members of the audience as to whether August 4th, 1914, fell on a Monday or a Tuesday. Each party presents apparently unassailable facts to support his argument. But having wisely accumulated more material than was strictly necessary for you to "get by" in your talk, you have reserves of information to draw upon. The fateful August 4th, 1914, was a Tuesday. That is just one instance of the kind of question you may be asked to settle. Memories are not always reliable, especially across the space of so many years—though you may find the questioner hard to convince on that point! Thorough and wide preparation means that you can quote authoritative documentary evidence, if necessary. There is no room for the kind of speaker who feels that he has no need of any particular preparation, and who trusts to the inspiration of the moment.

This chapter has been concerned with the gathering of suitable material for one particular kind of popular talk or lecture. The preparation of other popular types of addresses will be dealt with in later chapters. But whether the subject is local history of whatever, certain principles apply in each case.

First, it is necessary for you to get into your subject, and to get into it much further than is actually necessary for that particular talk.

The next step is to get your subject well into you—into your mind and memory.

You are then in a position to get your subject into your hearers.

Chapter 6

THE PARTS OF SPEECH

The title — the opening words — the middle — the conclusion.

EXCLUDING the title there are three obvious parts to a good speech—the introductory remarks; the middle, or body of the speech, and the closing remarks. Try to find an apt title, and one that sums up the main points of the talk. A good title arouses immediate interest and stirs curiosity. In the minimum number of words it tells people what to expect. The apt, eyecatching title is especially useful if your talk is to be advertised in the press, or on notice boards. Perhaps you have done some broadcasting, and you feel that people would be interested to hear of your experiences. A curiosity arousing title for such a talk would be "Behind the Scenes at the B.B.C." People like to be told what is going on in the regions beyond the public gaze. Another kind of title brings the prospective audience member into the picture. An expert on hygiene would attract a larger audience if he called his talk, "Food poisoning—and you!", rather than "The Necessity for Higher Standards of Hygiene." Your threefold aim in the matter of choosing a title is an honest indication of the contents of the talk, expressed in a manner calculated to arouse maximum interest, and using the minimum number of words.

The great moment arrives. The chairman has announced your name and the title of your talk, together with various more or less appropriate remarks about your character, qualifications and general background. You rise to your feet, remembering that good advice about addressing the people on the back row, where the hard of hearing invariably seem to congregate. "Mr. Chairman, ladies and gentlemen," or if you wish to be slightly less formal, "Mr. Chairman, and friends," you announce in clear, ringing tones. A quick look at the back row reveals an expression on their faces that says, "We'll hear this one without difficulty". Encouraged by this small initial success, you feel a little less nervous. You proceed to the real business. In the opening part of your speech you try to get on good terms with the audience, and at the same time tell them something of the scope of your talk, perhaps indicating what you intend to leave out, as well as what you will include. Getting on good terms with the audience may be accomplished by a reference to any local connection you may have. Your parents, or grand-parents, grew up there, or you did, or you worked in a local office, shop or factory at one time, or you were connected with a particular church, or you are still an admirer of the local football club. You want the audience to feel that you are one of them. References of this kind should be kept brief. Do not launch into a long string of reminiscences.

Alternatively, the chairman's remarks may give you a lead, even if it is only to correct some mis-statement he has made concerning you. Correct him in as kindly a manner as possible, smiling sweetly at him even though you are feeling distinctly irritated at his error.

A funny story, providing it has a definite bearing on the theme of the talk, and is not a "chestnut," puts the audience in an immediate good humour towards you. A joke, especially an old and feeble one, with no connection whatever with the theme in hand, may gain a laugh from the simpler members of the audience. But it will earn you the contempt and hostility of the intelligent people present. Asking a question, or if necessary two questions, is another effective

4

opening. A well received talk on hygiene began, "How many of you have suffered an attack of food poisoning during the past year?" Several hands were raised. The speaker continued, "How many of you have suffered what you called 'tummy upset' during the past twelve months?" The majority of the audience raised their hands.

A speaker has indeed a wide variety of styles of opening from which to select. We have noted several of them. According to your theme you could commence with a serious story, or with some item currently in the news, or with a topical quotation—an apt comment on today's conditions, or with words that immediately involve all present like, "You have come here tonight to find out. . . ." Your opening could be factual, perhaps a statistic with a human appeal. "While we are meeting here tonight . . . children will have died of starvation or malnutrition."

You could begin by saying "Thank you" to the chairman, or to the previous speaker, complimenting him on some point made especially clear. Or you could perhaps compliment the audience, or the town, on the newly and beautifully decorated hall in which you feel it a privilege to speak. Take your choice from this wide variety of opening remarks, according to the nature of your address, your audience and your temperament.

One thing you must never do in this opening (or any other) section of your speech. You must never tell the audience you really don't know why you have been invited to speak to them. This smacks of false modesty and insincerity, and the audience will recognise it as such right away. Be modest, by all means, but never apologise for your presence on the platform.

Although a good opening section is vital to the success of a speech, it should be kept short. Two minutes is quite enough for a speaker to get on good terms with his audience, and to indicate the scope of his talk. If you take much more than two minutes, some of the audience will become restless, as they ask themselves whether this fellow is ever going to get to the point.

Having obtained the goodwill and the interest of your audience, you now have the task of keeping them with you right to the last words of your talk. This you can do by presenting your facts in a logically arranged, coherent manner. Now is the time to bring out all those vivid instances, each in itself a weighty argument for whatever you are trying to convince them about. The speaker who is pleading for better standards of hygiene will bring out his and instances of dirty food shops, of kitchens of restaurants infested by mice, rats and cockroaches, of inconsiderate smokers who drop their ash over the food they are selling. After the evidence has been presented, in as colourful and down-to-earth style as possible, there comes the call to action. This could commence with a question, like, "What can *we* do to alter this intolerable situation?" In this instance the answer might be that we can all keep a watchful eye on those who prepare and serve our foodstuff, and report to the appropriate authority those who offend against the public interest by acting in a sloppy, irresponsible manner. Colourful anecdotes and descriptions supply a twofold purpose. They rest the hearers' minds in between the more closely reasoned parts of the talk, and they are the parts most easily remembered, and therefore more likely to make a permanent impression. Asking a relevant question from time to time, also maintains the interest, and stirs the mind inclined to be torpid. A striking phrase, repeated from time to time, also helps to keep interest alive. If your talk has "followed a charted course," your arguments arranged in a logical progression, the audience will still be with you, and you can move into the final section, where you aim to clinch the whole matter.

Do not under-estimate the importance of a good, strong

51

closing section, lest your talk tapers out feebly, or ends abruptly, leaving the audience "in the air". Give as much thought to the ending as you did to the beginning, for the ending sums up the whole matter, and in some cases challenges the audience to take some necessary action. Too long an ending has been compared to a guest taking too long to say "Good-bye." It arouses a feeling of impatience, even of boredom. How you end determines the impression, favourable or otherwise, you will leave with the audience. The good impression you created with the opening and the body of the speech can be thrown away by a weak ending.

An oldtime preacher summed up his method in the words, "First, I tells them what I'm going to tell them. Then I tells them. Then I tells them what I've told them." There is sound commonsense in this. In your opening words you told them something of the scope of your talk. In the middle section you elaborated on this. In the closing section it is a good idea to summarise the main points of the address. Thoughtful members of the audience will be grateful to you for this.

When you come to the end of the body of the speech, pause for a moment before you launch into the ending. This creates a feeling of anticipation that the end draws near. Do not begin the last section with words like, "Well, friends, I think that's about all I have to tell you," or worse still, "I think that's about all I know of this." A better way is to repeat the main headings of the talk, pausing a moment between each. Then a short and relevant story; or a fact, statistical or otherwise; or a verse of a poem, according to the nature and object of the speech. If your talk has been about a matter of social or national concern, you can end with a question confronting your hearers with a stark alternative, from which they have no option but to choose. You try to get them in a corner, and make them say "Yes" or "No"! The forms, or the subscription lists, are available at the back of the hall!

Again, according to the nature of your subject, you might end effectively with a quotation, maybe slightly adapted to your purpose. The speaker on the necessity for better standards of hygiene, of whom we have been thinking, could end by declaiming, with an air of pleasant authority, "The price of freedom—from being poisoned, as with any other matter—is eternal vigilance."

Some speakers end with a pious "God bless you," or even "God bless." If you are really sincere about it, this is no doubt, in order. But if it is only a gimmick, if you really do not think it makes the slightest difference whether God blesses the audience or not, then along with any other insincerities, it is better left out.

Avoid giving the audience the impression that you have almost finished, and then disappoint them by starting off on a new line of thought. Do not join the band of not so popular speakers who are known for their habit of "missing good stopping places." Thus rudely to dash your hearers' hopes is inexcusable, and is evidence of a lack of orderly planning on the speaker's part. A good speech is not a shapeless mass of possibly quite interesting facts and anecdotes, relevant to the subject, but set in no kind of logical order and progression. A test of a good speech, well delivered, is that a thoughtful member of the audience should be able to be able to outline the steps you took to lead your hearers to the desired conclusion.

Chapter 7

THE SHORTER SPEECHES

Weddings, toasts, votes of thanks, opening bazaars and fêtes, presenting prizes, after dinner, debates, impromptu, opening a discussion, open air.

IN this chapter we consider the occasions when short speeches are required. For our purposes we define a short speech as one taking up anything from two to twenty minutes.

Weddings and other Festive Occasions

Many a man has made his first halting attempt at public speaking as the best man, or the bridegroom, at a wedding reception. The time for speeches comes after the cutting of the bridal cake. If yours was a very stylish marriage you may have had six speeches.

A friend of the bridegroom's family proposed the health of the bride and groom.

The bridegroom replied.

A friend of the bride's family proposed the health of the bridesmaids.

The best man replied.

A friend of the bridegroom's family proposed the health of the host and hostess.

The bride's father replied.

That made six speeches. Let us hope they were all kept on the short side!

It is more usual to have three speeches only.

The bride's father, or some relative or close friend of the family, proposes the health and happiness of the bride and bridegroom. In Chapter 1 we indicated the kind of line

54

he usually takes.

The bridegroom then replies. His is essentially a "Thank you" speech. He thanks the bride's parents for having such a charming daughter, and for providing such an excellent meal. He thanks all the guests for their attendance, and everyone for the variety of presents received. He also thanks the bridesmaids for gracing the occasion so charmingly.

The best man replies briefly, on behalf of the bridesmaids, and then reads out the congratulatory telegrams. The bride's father ends his little speech by inviting the guests to rise, and to drink to the health and happiness of the happy couple. The bridegroom asks the guests to join him in drinking to the future happiness of the bridesmaids.

Those readers who are beginners in the art of public speaking can take comfort from the fact that no one expects a polished, professional performance, and that if you are really unaccustomed to speaking in public you have the sympathy of all present. In a nutshell the way to make a satisfactory speech at a wedding reception is—be short, be simple, be sincere. If you are feeling very nervous, and fear you may forget to mention some one, or something, you ought to mention, write out the key words on a card, just to jog your confused mind. A very nervous bridegroom, for instance, might write on his card, "Mother and father-in-law. Reception. Guests for coming. Presents. Bridesmaids." This would ensure he did not omit anyone he ought to thank, and would be better than writing out his speech in full, and then reading it. Read speeches lack the spontaneous and the informality which should be a feature of a wedding reception. The general rule about not apologising for shortcomings and deficiencies applies in this instance too. Do not tell them that you really do not know what to say, or that you are really no good as a speaker. Why labour these points, when they are probably already painfully apparent? If your throat feels very dry, it is in order for you to pause, and to take a sip of water, or other liquid. But it is bad manners to smoke while you are delivering your speech.

For other festive occasions, like coming of age parties, wedding anniversaries, or a party to mark someone's retirement from business or from public life, the same general rules apply. Be short. Be simple. Be sincere. Never try to get a cheap laugh at the expense of the married couple, the one come of age or the one who is retiring. Cut out any remark or joke which is in bad taste. Remember always that this is not your day, but his, hers or theirs!

Votes of Thanks

Many a man or woman has begun his, or her, career as a public speaker by proposing, or seconding, a vote of thanks to the main speaker or speakers, or to the organisers or to the ladies for providing refreshments at a meeting. It is part of a secretary's duty to find suitable people for these courtesies, and to find them before the meeting begins. When he has found them he should tell the chairman, so that the latter can call upon the two by name at the appropriate time in the meeting. If you are asked to propose or second the thanks it is helpful if you know something about both the speaker and his subject. If you are the proposer, do not talk for more than three minutes. For the seconder, two minutes is sufficient.

We have met proposers and seconders who could not think of any better opening words than, "Well, friends, I'm sure I don't know why I should be chosen to propose (or second) this vote of thanks. I don't know the speaker—never met him before tonight. And I know nothing about the subject . . ." He maunders on, and ends with "but I'm sure we all agree it's been a very nice talk, and we thank him for giving up his valuable time, and coming so far to talk to us here tonight. On behalf of one and all—thank you."

Neither the audience nor the speaker who is thanked is happy about this kind of effort. They conclude that the secretary was either desperate, or else completely lacking in gumption to have asked such an incompetent person. Begin, "Mr. Chairman, I have much pleasure in proposing a vote of thanks to our speaker." Then tell of any special reason why you have been chosen for the task. You were at school with the speaker, or he was your teacher, or you were his teacher, or you worked together at one time, or you have been interested in his subject for many years past. Go on to make some comment on the contents of his speech, and on the way he delivered it. Do not criticise the speaker, and do not put forward your own opinions. Include a laugh, if possible, but never at the speaker's expense. If the speaker has simply done the job he is being paid to do, there is no occasion to go into raptures about how good it is of him to spare valuable time, and as we all know he is *such* a busy man, and yet, he has come all this way to talk to us tonight! An exception to this rule is when a speaker, at some inconvenience to himself, has filled in at short notice for the advertised speaker who has, perhaps, been taken ill.

Pick out one or two especially good points in the speech, and comment briefly upon them. Only very rarely is a speech delivered of which it is impossible to find anything good to say! In that rare event the honest and kindly proposer should simply say, "Mr. Chairman, I propose that our thanks be given to the speaker," and leave it at that!

The seconder may find that the proposer has touched on the very points that impressed him too. If he is quite unable, at such short notice, to find anything fresh to say, he should underline what the proposer has said. Then he can say, "Mr. Chairman, I have much pleasure in seconding this vote of thanks," and sit down.

57

Beginners are sometimes tempted to write out their little speeches of thanks, and either to read them out, or to recite them in a stilted manner. "Mr. Chairman, we are very grateful to Mr. So-and-so for coming along tonight, and for giving us such an inspiring and informative speech." These efforts give pleasure to no one — not even the ones who make them. Proposing or seconding a vote of thanks, if taken seriously and done thoroughly, is good practice in the art of speaking and of thinking while on your feet. In the kindness of your heart, think of it as also doing a good turn to the speaker. He may be an experienced speaker, but he still needs encouragement and appreciation. This does not mean that you have to "lay it on thick," in your eulogies. The speaker is the one likely to be least deceived by exaggerations and insincerities, however well meant. A few simple, straightforward words, that show you have understood and appreciated what he said, is all that is necessary to send him away with a lighter heart than when he came. That kind of attitude on the part of the proposer and seconder can transform what sometimes degenerates into a routine formality into a piece of real service.

Opening Bazaars and Fêtes

"I will now call upon Mrs. Whats-her-name to declare this bazaar (fête, sale of work, Olde English Fayre) open," says the Vicar. You rise to your feet, and in the next not more than five minutes you tell them something about your interest and concern, and of any connection you may have, with the object of the effort. You will not lecture them at length about the excellences of the cause they have gathered to support, though a striking fact or two would not be out of place. If a target sum for the day has been set, you will mention that. You will not forget to praise the way in which the stalls and the hall have been decorated. And that is all that is necessary. Having touched briefly on these points you go on to say, "I have much pleasure in now declaring this bazaar open." An exception to the five minute maximum rule is if you are a celebrity who is being paid handsomely for this little job. If you do not entertain them for a little longer than five minutes the people will complain, quite rightly, that you have not earned your money.

Presenting the Prizes

Children, and young people generally, can be either the best or the worst of audiences. To talk to an audience of intelligent, responsible teenagers who are eager to learn, is one of the most satisfying experiences a speaker can have. But bore them, talk down to them, and they will not conceal their feelings as adults will, and unless you are quite insensitive you will sit down as quickly as you can. They are also very quick to detect any insincerity on the part of the speaker. So, if you are invited to present the prizes at the local school you face a big and worthwhile task. There they sit, row on row, hundreds of them, their ages ranging from perhaps eleven up to seventeen. That wide age range in itself presents a problem. Your task may be made all the more difficult because they may have already listened to a long and perhaps dull and prosy report from the head teacher. They may be already restless when you rise to make your speech before presenting the prizes.

On no account tell them that hoary old falsehood about schooldays being the happiest days of our lives! If this is so, then they have nothing to which they can look forward with anticipation. Seventeen years of age, and the best of life already over! What nonsense! And what an insult to our marriage partner—I was happiest before I met you! If you never won any prizes at school there is no need for you to boast about it now, as though it were a matter of some credit.

Begin your speech, "Mr. Chairman, and school . . ." Do not call them children, nor even girls and boys, lest you create an initial unfavourable impression on the great

59

majority of them, for they like to think that they are grown up. The particular line your address will take depends upon local circumstances, and upon what you are, and what you know. If you have a suitable anecdote, tell it early on in the address, before their attention has a chance to flag. On the actual line of your talk, it is a good thing to do a little detective work beforehand, to find out something about their studies and other activities. Was there a school trip to Paris? If you had an interesting experience, or have a tale to tell of some historic happening in one of those parts, they will listen. One speaker, enquiring about subjects being studied, discovered that many of his hearers had been reading the works of R. L. Stevenson, including "Treasure Island". As a basis for his address he used a sentence from the last page of that rumbustious romance.

"All of us had an ample share of the treasure, and used it wisely or foolishly, according to our nature." Life is largely what you care to make of it, so it's up to you, was his theme.

If you have had any experience of social work you could warn them about some of the dangers and pitfalls of contemporary life. You could perhaps tell them something of the real purpose of education, or of the difference made by the attitude we take up towards life. Whatever you tell them, keep the human element well to the fore, driving home the points you wish to make by quoting actual instances. Congratulate the prizewinners, complimenting them on all the hard work they must have put in. At the same time remind them, and those who have not won prizes, that school prizes are no guarantee of success in later life. Whether or not they are prizewinners now, success still means much hard work later. Whatever line you decide to take, be sure to come to the end of it within twenty minutes.

After Dinner Speeches

You have been asked to propose, or to respond to, a toast at the annual dinner of some society in which you are interested. First, make yourself quite clear about what or whom you are toasting or replying on behalf. Are you toasting the future progress and prosperity of the society and its work, or are you replying on behalf of the ladies? Being quite clear on this point you can proceed to gather your material. How much material will you need? That will depend upon the number of toasts to follow the dinner. If there are several, it will be sufficient for you to make one point clearly, and then to sit down. As a general rule three toasts, in addition to "The Queen", are thought sufficient. The first toast is always, "The Queen", proposed by the chairman, without any speech. If the following toasts are limited to three, or less, your speech should not, even then, exceed 15 minutes.

After dinner speeches are traditionally lighthearted, humorous and friendly. Listeners look forward to being entertained, but this does not put you under the obligation of telling a succession of more or less funny stories. The contents of your speech will vary according to the character of your fellow diners—youth club, students, businessmen or women, church members, old soldiers, sportsmen or whatever. A lighthearted story, preferably one they have never heard before; a hard core of facts, and an absence of platitudes make a good after dinner speech. And, if you are the proposer, by inviting your audience to stand and to drink with you.

And the Golden Rule here, as with any other kind of speech, is to put yourself in the place of your listeners, and to ask if anything you say is likely to grate upon or embarrass. If you are in any doubt about any point on this score, cut it out.

Debates

The debate is a good training ground for potential public

61

speakers. In the cut and thrust you develop the ability to think, and to speak, clearly. You learn to take into account the other person's point of view, and you begin to realise the many sided nature of truth. All these are essential assets for the public speaker. Procedure at debates is modelled on that of the House of Commons. There is a chairman, who presides impartially, whatever his personal views and feelings on the subject being debated. He calls upon the proposer to state the motion, and to present the case FOR. When the proposer has done his best the opposer states the case AGAINST. The seconder of the motion then rises and gives the audience the benefit of his opinions, and he is followed by the seconder for the opposition. Before the vote is taken there is a general discussion, which provides the absolute beginner in public speaking with an opportunity to commence his training.

An experienced speaker will be ready to propose or oppose, whatever his own personal feelings on the subject debated. But the beginner, if asked to propose or oppose would be wise to agree to speak only for the side with which he personally agrees.

Proposer and seconder should come together before the debate, and agree on what line each is to take, and what argument and facts each is to put forward. Do not try to give exhaustive treatment to the subject, or you will probably exhaust the patience of the audience at the same time. Deliberately leave some things unsaid, in order to stimulate questions and discussions. But take good care that your knowledge of the subject includes those unsaid matters. Put yourself in the place of an imaginary awkward critic who is looking for flaws in your presentation of the case, and try to forestall him. Avoid dubious generalisations like, "as everybody knows", or "everybody agrees", thereby inviting the critic to jump to his feet with a formidable list of exceptions to your glib statement. Look carefully at the evidence you produce to support your case. Could the fact you state be used equally well to advance the opposition's arguments? Check your facts and figures, and be ready to quote your authority for stating them; at the same time making sure that they are the latest available. And be quite sure to give a definite "Yes", or "No" to the proposition according to which side you represent. There is no room in the cut and thrust of a debate for the neutrals or the "Don't knows." Your aim is to persuade listeners to vote for your views.

Courtesy will prevent you from trying to ridicule your opponent. Your ridicule, if any, will stop short at the views he is presenting. In any case, ridicule can prove a double-edged weapon, so be sparing in the use you make of it. A wiser approach might be to take your opponent's views, and then to say, "But I find certain difficulties in accepting such ideas," and then go on to explain why this should be so.

Well chosen facts, well marshalled arguments and keeping within a twenty minute limit—these are the keys to success in debate.

Impromptu Speeches

A good definition of an impromptu speech is one that is made without at least ten minutes notice, and that is not a repeat of a former speech. Impromptu speeches can be heard in a debate, when the proposer or opposer is exercising his right to reply. Many votes of thanks, responses to toasts and replies in "Any Questions" sessions are instances of impromptu speeches. Obviously, if you are "dropped on" at a moment's notice you cannot reasonably be expected to produce as good a result as if you had been given time for adequate preparation. Hence the late Lord Birkett's judgement that most impromptu speeches are not worth the paper they were not written on. Take comfort from the fact that, in these cases, your hearers do not expect anything great in the way of oratory. If the chairman un-expectedly calls upon you to "say a few words", or to "voice our thanks" to some one or other, do not panic, but play for time, while you gather your thoughts. Rising slowly to your feet, you could take off and polish your spectacles, at the same time saying, "Well, Mr. Chairman, you've certainly taken me by surprise . . . ," and then continue with such thoughts as have by now come into your mind.

The best impromptu speeches are those which are not really impromptu at all. The speaker has suspected that he might be called upon, and has prepared his mind, just in case. Herein lies the force of Mark Twain's saying that it usually took him three weeks to prepare a good impromptu speech; The more time you have been able to spend on the preparation of your impromptu speech the more spon-taneous it should sound. Intelligent anticipation is the key to an effective impromptu speech. But if the worst happens, and you are completely taken by surprise, console yourself with the thought that nobody really expects anything great, in those circumstances, anyway!

Opening a Discussion

A generation or two ago audiences were more content to listen to a long address, and then to disperse, than is the case today. The modern audience prefers a shorter talk, and ample time for questions and discussion. Many of us are unwilling to accept, without question, just what we are told, or what has been handed down to us. Hence the popularity of the discussion group, or the discussion period at the end of a lecture. The aim of a discussion is not to display our deep and wide knowledge of a subject, nor to win a victory over an opponent. It is to broaden the knowledge of all present, by making clear opposing viewpoints, and leaving all who take part with a deeper knowledge and insight into the topic than when they began the discussion.

When you are asked to open a discussion the very first thing to remember is just that. You have not been asked to give an exhaustive and definitive address, but an impartial indication of different approaches to the problem, together with some facts that will form a basis for intelligent discussion. Ten minutes, or a quarter of an hour at the most, is ample for your introduction. Go beyond that, and people will justly complain that they did not come to listen to a lecture, and that you had left them with so much the less for them to say. In order to compile your opening you will have accumulated enough material to last you for half an hour or more. Keep it in reserve. Points will arise in the discussion when appeals for further information will be made to you. If you have told them all you know in your short introductions, then you will look rather foolish when points keep arising and you can give no guidance whatever. To open a discussion may not, indeed should not, take more than ten minutes. But it can involve you in as much preparation as for an address lasting half an hour.

In the Open Air

If you are called upon to speak in the open air, let us hope that a microphone is available. This removes all strain on the vocal cords. If no such modern mechanical aid is at hand, insist on speaking downwind, if you wish to be heard; and try to get your audience as close as possible to you. An open air audience tends to be a constantly changing audience, rather than a captive one such as we address in halls. While some will stay for the whole of the session, you can also expect a constant drift of others to and from the crowd. You will adapt your tactics accordingly. Aim at crystal clarity, making two or three points, if possible linked with some current happening, or some very recent news in the papers and on the radio and

65

television.

Open air speakers resort to various devices to warm up, and to sustain the interest. Provided you know the answers you can ask questions. Or you can arrange with a friend to ask a question, or even to indulge in a little heckling. If you have the opportunity, study the regular open air speakers, and their methods. A visit to Tower Hill, or to Speakers' Corner, in Hyde Park, can be illuminating. Listen to a man like Lord Soper, probably Britain's most effective open air speaker, as he answers the varied hotch-potch of questions thrown at him. Note how he is making, not one, but a whole series of little speeches as he deals faithfully with the remarkable variety of points raised by his hearers. Note how he pricks the fallacy contained in many of the questions addressed to him; how he some-times turns the question back on the questioner, and makes him answer his own question; how he combines forth-rightness with good humour not to mention his encyclopedic knowledge of so many subjects. Open air speaking is not so popular as it once was, but it still fulfills a certain, though diminished, public need.

Chapter 8

THE PERFECT CHAIRMAN

The chairman's addresses — only part of his duty — controlling the meeting — helping the main speaker(s).

THIS chapter is, in one way, a continuation of the previous chapter, for part of the chairman's duty is to deliver short speeches. But, as we shall see, speaking may be only part of your duties if you accept an invitation to preside over a public meeting.

A good chairman sets out to do everything within his power to ensure that the speaker, or speakers, of the evening will have the maximum opportunity to attain whatever is the object of their coming. The chairman is always second in importance to the main speaker, or speakers. His job is to prepare the way for them. He will arrive in good time, and not bustle in a minute before the proceedings are due to commence. Tactfully he will check up on whether people like the secretary and the caretaker have done their jobs properly. Are the lighting, ventilation and heating in good order? If people's feet are cold they find it difficult to listen attentively to the most fascinating of speakers. If the hall is stuffy the audience will find it so much easier to doze off. Where is the speaker positioned? It is more difficult to make every one hear, and to hold their attention, if you speak from the middle of the long side of a hall. Has a reading desk, or lectern, been provided for the speaker? A tall speaker, provided with only a low table on which to place his notes, is at a disadvantage. Has a glass of fresh water been provided, in case the speaker's throat goes dry? If there is reason to believe that the hall will not be filled, a tactful word to the stewards might result in the front rows being filled first. A speaker is not exactly helped by having to speak across a forest of empty seats to an audience who have placed themselves as far away as possible from him. If flowers have been provided the chairman will see that they are not so positioned as to hide the speaker's face.

Having checked up on these mundane, but necessary matters, the chairman will be at hand to welcome the speaker, when he arrives, and to give him any necessary information about the premises and the meeting. He will tell the speaker that if he sees any people leaving early, it is not because they can endure no more talk from him, but because they have a bus or train to catch, or maybe are going on to another meeting. He will tell the speaker if the room must be vacated at a certain time, of if the members are in the habit of closing the meeting by a certain hour. If questions and discussion are the rule, he will tactfully suggest that the speaker leaves time for the members of the audience to have their say. If there are acoustical problems, he will inform the speaker of them, at the same time passing on any hints on how best to deal with them.

A good chairman will not expect the speaker to make small talk before a meeting—unless, of course, the speaker shows a desire to discuss the state of the weather or of the local football team. At about two minutes before the appointed hour for the meeting to commence the chairman will usher the platform party, if any, on to the platform. He will seat the speaker on his right hand. If there are two speakers he will seat one on either side of him. Having attended to all these matters he will then start the meeting at the duly appointed hour.

Bearing in mind that he is there to prepare the way for

the speaker the chairman will welcome the audience, and then introduce the person they have come to hear in words like these:

"Ladies and gentlemen: As our speaker this evening we welcome the Rev. John Jones, of Westhampton. Mr. Jones' subject is, 'The Colour Problem in the Midlands.' Mr. Jones is well qualified to deal with his subject. For the past four years he has worked in an area where there are thousands of immigrants. Before that he worked for ten years in the West Indies. Mr. Jones is the author of the book, "Commonsense and the Colour Bar," which some of us have read, and found very illuminating. Last week some of us listened to Mr. Jones taking part in a discussion of the colour question on the radio. In this part of the world it would be difficult to find a man better qualified to talk to us on this contemporary problem than our speaker tonight. We are indeed fortunate to have him with us. Ladies and gentlemen: the Rev. John Jones."

Any speaker would be pleased with such an introduction. The chairman gave him his correct name and title. He did not fall into the common error of addressing him, or of referring to him, as "the Rev. Jones." He called him "the Rev. John Jones," or "Mr. Jones," as circumstances dictated. He gave the audience full information about the speaker's excellent qualifications for talking to them on that particular subject. He stressed the fact that the speaker knew his subject well enough to be able to write a book about it. In fact the speaker was regarded as sufficiently high authority on his subject to be invited to discuss it on the radio. The chairman portrayed this speaker in the most favourable light possible to his audience. A good chairman creates a good impression of the speaker. This he does, not by flattery, but by simply stating facts with which he has gone to the trouble of acquainting himself before the meeting. Plain unadorned facts have a way of speaking for themselves, quite independently of flowery compliments.

Note also the strict impartiality of the chairman. We are left in complete darkness about the chairman's own views on the colour problem. For all the audience knows his views may be the complete opposite of those of the speaker. On the other hand, he may know no more than the average member of the audience. In any case, he did not take up time airing his knowledge of the subject, perhaps relating anecdotes of coloured immigrants he had known, and of their difficulty in adapting to the British way of life. Nor did he try to steal the limelight by telling a succession of more or less funny, and more or less relevant stories. By his brevity such a chairman has set the tone for the meeting. In these instances brevity is next to godliness! Nor was there ever any doubt as to who was the principal speaker for the evening.

The chairman remains standing until the speaker has risen, and then sits down. He remains on the platform. The sight and sound of a chairman scuttling down to a seat in the audience, and then scuttling back as soon as the address is finished, is not helpful either to the speaker or to the audience. The chairman remains on the platform, where he is better placed to deal with any heckling or interruptions. If the necessity should arise he is also better placed to pull the speaker's coat if he is taking up more than his allotted time, and maybe encroaching on the next speaker's time. The chairman also sets the audience a good example by keeping his eyes on the speaker, and looking interested. He will not confer, in penetrating whispers, with the secretary or other members of the platform party, thereby distracting both speaker and audience. In case of any real necessity for such communication, he will achieve his purpose by silently passing a brief note, and he will do that as unobtrusively as possible.

His address finished, the speaker sits down. The chairman

rises and if there is to be a session of questions and comments indicates that the meeting is now open for contributions from the floor. If a prolonged and painful silence follows, the chairman can put a question of h.s own, which he has brought along just in case such an emergency should arise. On the other hand, if the speaker has been provocative, three people may jump to their feet simultaneously with their questions. The chairman will then indicate the order in which they are to speak. He will insist that all questions and comments are addressed to the chairman, and will call to order any persons who indulge in an exchange of opinions across the hall. There are bad mannered people who talk, often loudly, to one another, instead of to the chairman. They make it difficult for the man who is observing the courtesies by address'ng the chairman. Neither the chairman nor the speaker, nor other members of the audience can hear him properly against a bad mannered babble of talk from the less courteous members of the audience. The chairman will call them to order, perhaps asking them to give the benefit of their remarks to the whole company, instead of to their immediate neighbours only.

The chairman must use his discretion about allowing just what questions may be put. His guide line is, "Is this question really relevant to the subject?" If not, he will declare it out of order. He will also call to order any person who interprets the opportunity to ask a question, or to make a comment, as an invitation to make a speech. If some one, in order to gain a laugh, or to embarrass the speaker, asks a really silly question, the chairman will smile benevolently, and reply, "Come now, let's be serious."

If the speaker has really aroused the feelings of the meeting there may be a demand for action. This might call for some knowledge of the rules of debate on the part of the chairman. He is now responsible for ensuring that the

71

feeling of the meeting is properly ascertained in regard to the matter before them.

A member of the audience may rise and say, "Mr. Chairman, I propose that we send a letter from this meeting to the local Member of Parliament, deploring the lack of interest shown by the government in the immigrant population of this area." The chairman asks, "Is there a seconder?" If no one thinks the resolution is worth seconding the resolution falls to the ground, and the matter is closed. But if a seconder is forthcoming, relevant discussion is allowed until the audience is ready to vote on the proposition. The chairman reads out the motion, "That a letter be sent from this meeting, to the local Member of Parliament, deploring the lack of interest shown by the government in the immigrant population of this area." He then asks those in favour to raise their right hands, and after that those who are against the resolution to do the same. He declares the result in the words, "The motion is carried," or "The motion is lost," as the case may be.

But matters do not always work out so simply as that, hence the need for some knowledge of the rules of debate. When the meeting is open for discussion a member of the audience may propose an amendment — or what he thinks is an amendment. An amendment must not only be relevant to the motion, but it must amend it — not contradict it. An amendment may therefore add words or omit words, or substitute words for those in the original resolution. So, if someone rises and says, "Mr. Chairman, I propose that we do NOT send a letter to the local Member of Parliament," the chairman at once rules him out of order, explaining that what he has proposed is a direct negative, and that he can obtain the result he desires by voting against the proposition.

Someone else rises and says, "Mr. Chairman, I propose an amendment — that we send a deputation to the local

Member of Parliament, instead of the proposed letter." He wishes to substitute the word "deputation" for the word "letter" in the original proposition. That is in order, and if a seconder is forthcoming the chairman puts the amendment to the meeting. If it is carried it becomes the substantive motion, superceding the original motion. As such it must be put to the vote. This is usually a formality, as those who voted for the amendment are unlikely to vote against it immediately afterwards. As it was carried first only as an amendment, it must be carried a second time before it can be passed as a resolution.

Let us suppose that this amendment was lost, and we are back at the original proposition to send a letter. Somebody rises and proposes an amendment to the effect that copies of the letter be sent to the Home Secretary and to the Prime Minister. As an addition to the original proposition this is in order. If it is seconded the proposition, which the chairman reads out, becomes, "That a letter be sent from this meeting to the local Member of Parliament, and copies of the letter to the Home Secretary and to the Prime Minister, deploring the lack of interest shown by the government in the immigrant population of this area." The chairman puts the matter to the meeting, and they either accept or reject it as they feel inclined.

Someone else may feel that the amended resolution, as it stands, is not strong enough, and therefore proposes to add a rider. An amendment varies or amplifies a resolution. A rider adds a material relevant fact. In this case the rider might take some such form as the addition of some such words as, "and calls upon the government to take immediate action." Riders are dealt with by the chairman in the same way as amendments.

If the discussion drags on, and the audience begins to weary of the flood of words, any member of the gathering may propose the Previous Question. This is a form of closure, very useful to check those who are intoxicated by the exuberance of their own verbosity. It generally means, "that the question be not now put." The chairman is bound to put the question to the meeting at once. If it is carried, it gets rid of the motion before the meeting. If it is negatived, the main question must be put at once. Either way the verbose ones are checked, and the question before the meeting resolved one way or another, and forthwith, with no further delay.

Complications like these do not arise very often, but the possibility of their doing so cannot be ruled out. Hence the desirability of a chairman having some acquaintance with the rules of debate, lest he finds himself in a real tangle, struggling confusedly with amendments to amendments, or even with amendments to amendments to amendments! If the chairman finds himself out of his depth, let us hope that a knowledgeable secretary is at hand to guide him on to firm ground!

Whether there were questions, discussion and resolutions, or not, the meeting ends with a vote of thanks to the speakers and others connected with the organisation of the meeting — the trustees of the hall, the ladies who will serve the refreshments, and to the chairman for the way he has presided over and guided the meeting to its desired end. The chairman calls, first upon the proposer, and then the seconder, of the vote of thanks. When they have had their say, the chairman may add a complimentary sentence of his own, perhaps filling in something they have omitted, and then calls on all who are in favour to show it in the usual way.

If refreshments are served the chairman does not leave the speaker high and dry on the platform, while he joins his friends in the audience. He stays with the speaker, and his friends join them. It is unkind of a chairman to abandon a speaker among a lot of strangers, supposing that somebody will go and talk to him. It is part of the chairman's job, for he stands towards the speaker in the relation of host. If the chairman has really urgent business with someone in the audience he should arrange for a friend to keep company with the speaker in his unavoidable absence.

All public meetings are by no means so exacting upon the chairman as the one we have described. Many others are much more homely affairs, often taking place upon church premises. You may be asked to preside over a weekend church anniversary meeting, or at a musical evening where you are expected to announce the various items. On these occasions, in addition to being asked to introduce the speakers or musicians, an item on the programme asks for "Chairman's Remarks," or "Chairman's Address." This gives the chairman an opportunity of showing himself at one with the audience, and of saying encouraging things to them. But everyone is hoping that these remarks or this address will be brief. Ten minutes is usually more than enough. Twenty minutes is a crime. The chairman at these meetings needs to bear in mind that he is of secondary importance. The people have come to listen to the advertised speaker, or to the singers and instrumentalists, and not to him. If he is unwilling to make the speaker, or the musicians, and not himself, the centre of attention, he should not have accepted the invitation to preside.

In a debate it is the chairman's duty to make sure that the audience knows exactly what it is that they are asked to decide. The chairman states the point at issue as lucidly as he can, before putting it to the vote. If any speaker goes on at undue length, the chairman will restrain him. After the voting the chairman compliments the losing side on the brave show they have made, and congratulates the winners.

At a dinner the chairman proposes the first toast, "The Queen," but makes no speech. He introduces those who propose and respond to the other toasts in a sentence or two, bringing out their connection with the occasion.

What qualities go to the making of a perfect chairman? Often chairmen are chosen because they are Very Important Persons. This, in itself may be an initial disadvantage. If one is conscious that one is a V.I.P., one finds it all the harder to attain that degree of self-effacement necessary, because the speaker in a meeting is definitely a more important person than the chairman. A degree of humility and self-effacement is part of the make-up of the ideal chairman.

Humility does not imply weakness, that the chairman is a doormat. On the contrary a good chairman will manage the meeting without at all appearing to be "managing". He will dominate without giving the impression that he is domineering. He will control without creating the impression that he is dictating the course of the proceedings. The perfect chairman is that very rare person the benevolent autocrat.

At the same time he creates the feeling that he is impartial and that under his chairmanship everyone will be given part of a chairman's duty is to maintain the right of free speech. Everyone can have his say — though it is impossible for everyone to have his way! The chairman no doubt has his own personal opinions and feelings about the matter under discussion, but he keeps those opinions and feelings to himself while he is occupying the chair.

Since most audiences contain at least one awkward, obstreperous person with a chip on his shoulder, the chairman needs to be a person of tact and patience. At the same time he must be firm to call to order anyone who makes a remark in bad taste, or who makes a personal attack on the speaker or any other member of the audience. An occasional flash of humour, without being merely silly or facetious, helps to dispel any tension which may be building up. But it must be kindly, genial humour, not sarcasm, or sick, or black humour In extreme cases, if tact, patience and good humour fail to restrain a person who is upsetting the meeting, the chairman must ask him to withdraw. If he defies the chairman, the stewards may remove h.m, using a reasonable degree of force. Fortunately such instances are very rare. A wise chairman ignores minor interruptions, but if they continue he appeals to the audience's sense of fair play and good sense. He will refrain from scolding the audience, and do all he can to keep them in good humour with the speaker, themselves and himself.

When the meeting is open for questions, discussions and propositions, and the air is thick with proposals, counter-proposals, amendments and riders, he will remain calm, and insist on one matter at a time commanding the attention of the meeting. If he really does feel out of his depth his humility will show itself in his not being ashamed to ask the guidance of the secretary, or any other knowledge-able person present. None of us is infallible, and none of us has an encyclopedic knowledge of any and every subject. There is nothing in the least to be ashamed of in acknowledging this. Under ideal conditions the chairman would know the subject under discussion better than, or at least as well as, anyone in the room or hall. This would make his task so much easier, especially if he is called upon to give guidance on any point. Knowing his subject thoroughly gives the chairman a feeling of confidence, and this communicates itself to the audience.

Yet another advantage is that the chairman is himself an experienced speaker. This gives him a sympathy with, and an understanding of, the task that faces the speaker of the evening. No chairman whose heart is in the right place, and who is also a practised speaker, would see a fellow speaker without proper provision for his notes, nor without a glass of water to moisten a dry throat; nor would he

77

introduce him in a perfunctory, almost curt manner which suggested a complete lack of interest in the speaker's background and qualifications; nor would he, at refreshment time, leave the speaker to drink his cup of tea in discourteous isolation.

Humble and self-effacing, yet always in control of the meeting; perhaps holding strong views on the subject under discussion, yet impersonal and impartial while he occupies the chair; patient, tactful, goodhumoured, yet very firm, even stern, if occasion demands; knowledgeable, yet not too proud to ask for guidance when the extent of his knowledge is reached; thoughtful and sympathetic towards the needs of the speaker — these are the qualities that go towards the making of the ideal chairman. To all these we might add that he is at all times dignified, without being pompous.

It may be objected that all this is an impossible counsel of perfection. Whoever met a chairman with all the qualities described in this chapter? This one is genial and tactful, but he allows garrulous ones to prolong the proceedings unnecessarily. That one, for all his good points, leads us to suspect that he is not always quite impartial in his judgments. Another one finds difficulty in controlling the meeting, allowing members of the audience to address their remarks to one another, instead of exclusively to the chairman. We do indeed meet some poor specimens of chairmen from time to time! In many cases the chairman fails because he has no clear idea of all that is required of him. If he had, he would rise to the occasion in a much more satisfactory manner. To know what constitutes perfection does not enable us to achieve perfection. But if the will is there it will ensure that we come so much closer to perfection than if we were vague and hazy about the whole matter.

78

Chapter 9

THE LONGER SPEECHES

Their construction — the lecture — types of lecture — literary, informative, experience, "how to" — holding the interest to the end.

FOR practical purposes we have defined the shorter speech as any public utterance taking less than twenty minutes. Some may ask whether, nowadays, there is any demand for talks that go on for more than one third of an hour. Past generations, without benefit of television, radio or cinema, revelled in listening to speeches that carried on for an hour, sometimes more, sometimes on what seem to us rather forbidding subjects. Lord Hugh Cecil, for instance, on one occasion held his fellow Parliamentarians "rivetted in pin-drop silence," for more than an hour, while he discoursed on the difference between Erastians and High Churchmen. But that was in the far distant past, in the world that passed away forever in 1914. Twenty minutes is enough for modern listeners — so some say. The fact of the matter is that, at numerous luncheons, speeches go on for up to forty minutes, and evening talks and lectures up to an hour, or even more. But if you are to hold the interest for that time you have to be good! If you are a luncheon speaker you will be asked to bear in mind that most of your listeners are due back at business by a certain time, and therefore a rigid time limit must be imposed on your oratory. But at evening meetings, where no such limitation is necessary, speakers can, and do, hold on for up to an hour. What is more, if they know their business, they can retain attention for that time, and even leave their listeners still wanting more.

Longer speeches are sometimes referred to as lectures. A lecture means a period of instruction. "To lecture" also carries a meaning of reproof. With undertones like these, to call your offering a lecture might be offputting to an audience of young people. Call it a talk, and they will lap it up — though you may not have altered a single word! Older people do not usually re-act so unfavourably to the word "lecture," especially the more thoughtful ones. Now let us go on to consider three of the most popular types of longer speeches, addresses, lectures, talks — what you will.

In spite of the strong competition of television a visit to any public library will convince that people are still reading lots of books. A story by some modern or oldtime author, portrayed on the little screen, will send many people back to the original. Hence the literary talk, especially if there is a topical link, is still appreciated. Jane Austen, the Brontës, Dickens, Bernard Shaw, H. G. Wells and many others — their works portrayed on the little screen attract viewers by the hundred thousand, maybe by the million. Many of these viewers would be interested to hear more about these authors, the kind of people they were, their domestic circumstances, and the lasting influence, if any, that they exerted.

Let us suppose you choose the late H. G. Wells, perhaps the most prolific and influential author since Dickens. What a wealth of human interest there is in the life story of this prophet, this pioneer of science fiction, this educationalist, who through his novels and other writings tried to prod the human race along what he thought was the road to their salvation! In your opening section you could dwell upon the poverty of his early life, and his apprenticeship to the drapery trade. You could point out the lasting influence on his life and work of these early experiences. The idea of people fighting to climb out of the rut of a constricted life, handicapped by ignorance and illiteracy, held a deep fascination for him. It comes up again and again in his books, notably in his novels, "Kipps," and "Mr. Polly." In Wells' own life the key to escape was education. Scientific education he believed to be the key to all human progress. Another section of your talk could deal with Wells, the scientist and prophet. You could refer to his pioneer science fiction story, "The Time Machine," and to some of the remarkable prophecies contained in some of his other scientific romances, like "The First Men in the Moon"; "This World Set Free," with its forecast of the atomic bomb; and "The Shape of Things to Come," prophesying the outbreak of the Second World War in Poland, about 1940. You could contrast the optimism of his earlier days with the near despair of his old age. How did it come about that this optimistic young writer of genius died an embittered, disappointed old man? Where did he go wrong in his beliefs and thinking?

These are but some of the points on which you could touch in your lecture on H. G. Wells. You would make your selection according to the nature of your audience. Wells the historian, the author of the monumental "Outline of History" is another facet you might display. If you are addressing a meeting connected with the Church you could describe Wells' early rejection of Christianity, his brief return to belief in the First World War, when he wrote, "God, the Invisible King," and his second and lasting rejection, at the same time giving Wells' own reasons for his attitude. If you are in any doubt about sources of information for your lectures, the local librarian will recommend, and if necessary, obtain for you the necessary books. In the case of H. G. Wells, the great man's autobiography will supply the basic information necessary.

Whatever literary figure you may choose it is wise to bear in mind that most people are interested more in people than in ideas. So keep the human element well to the fore. The reading of short, well chosen extracts from the writings of the subject of your lecture adds to the interest — a sample of the delights that await the reader. The opening paragraphs of Wells' "The History of Mr. Polly" come to mind as one piece of very fine writing. But keep the extracts short, and as few as may be necessary. Your reward for giving a lecture like this may be the knowledge that you have introduced people to new ideas, a new source of pleasure, and the consequent enrichment of their lives.

A second kind of popular talk deals with some experience in the life of the speaker. People are always interested in other people's experience of life. They are interested in other people's jobs. Sometimes they envy those whom they feel, have a "softer" job than they do, for example, the parson, whom some believe preaches twice on a Sunday, and then takes the rest of the week off! Speakers talking about their work not only pass a pleasant hour with their listeners, but broaden ideas and sympathies, and perhaps supply a wholesome corrective to nonsensical notions. There is no necessity that you hold some startlingly unusual way of earning your living before you attempt this kind of talk. If you are a school teacher, a nursing sister, a solicitor, an estate agent, a newspaper editor, a probation officer, a shop steward, a sanitary inspector or indeed hold any job that brings you into contact with people, then people will be interested to hear about your working hours, and what is expected of you then. If you are a housewife, and your husband is some public figure, constantly on call, like a doctor or a clergyman, you may have some interesting experiences to relate.

A talk of this kind, informal though it may be, still requires form and shape. It should not consist of a long string of vaguely related anecdotes and facts, set in no particular order. It could take the form of an account of

82

a typical day in the life of whatever kind of public servant or businessman or woman you happen to be. Or it could enumerate the different categories of work performed, with an account of each. At all times you would, of course, be careful not to betray any confidences, nor reveal any private information.

It may be that your daily work is of a nature that does not lend itself to a colourful talk. In that case your leisure time activities might form the subject of an interesting address. Do you belong to some community-serving organisation like Toc-H, the Rotary Club or the Women's Royal Voluntary Service? If so, people will be interested to hear about the good work in which you share. Tell them how you came to be connected with the cause in the first place, as well as about the services you are now rendering. Keep the personal note well to the fore, though at the same time not disclosing anything that ought not to be disclosed, say about the identity of people who are receiving benefits.

People like town councillors and magistrates have interesting tales to tell about their form of unpaid voluntary community service. Failing these leisure-time activities perhaps your hobby is freelance writing, in which you have had some modest success; or you may have done some broadcasting, and therefore feel qualified to give a talk about what happens behind the scenes at the B.B.C. before the speaker finds his way to the microphone. Or you may engage in some even less usual form of leisure-time activity, say as a prison visitor. You could then speak about the problems you encounter there, about the after-care of discharged prisoners, and your ideas about the causes of crime.

Under the heading of "experience" comes the travel talk. It is then a decided advantage if you bring in visual aids, a subject we shall deal with in the chapter on "The Illustrated Lecture". If no visual aid is available a good speaker can still hold the attention of the audience with an account of his visit to, or prolonged stay in, foreign parts. The late Gladys Aylward, the London parlourmaid who became a missionary in China, would hold the attention of large audiences for an hour at a time as she described her adventures and drew her conclusions.

The scope for the "experience" type of talk is extremely wide. "Real life" makes a constant appeal. If you are wondering about a suitable line for a talk you have been invited to give, the answer may well be in describing some aspect of your life in which other people could take an interest.

A third kind of popular address is the "how to" talk, with or without some form of visual demonstration. Subjects like cookery and embroidery and the like are obviously more effectively communicated if the lecturer is also a demonstrator. But there are plenty of subjects in this category which can be given in the form of a plain, unadorned talk.

The gardener can pass on all kinds of helpful hints on how to grow bigger and better vegetables, and larger, more colourful blooms.

The marriage guidance expert can tell his hearers how to ensure that they make their union a happy and fruitful one, by pointing out the various pitfalls, and telling how to avoid them.

The police officer can tell how to make our homes, if not burglar proof, at least more difficult for the burglar to enter.

The beautician can instruct the Young Wives, and maybe the older wives too, on how to preserve their facial and other charms.

Many young parents have a secret fear that their offsprings may turn into juvenile delinquents. Even if you are not a professional child guidance expert, with all the very latest theories at your fingertips, but just an ordinary parent whose children have grown up, and "turned out well," you might be able to talk to the members of the Parent-Teacher Association on how to make a success of bringing up their children. It would help them to know that your little John or Mary, had tantrums and even stole things occasionally and then told lies about it, just like their children do now. An effective, homely talk on how to bring up children could be given from the angle of their needs. You could divide the talk into four sections — every child's need for affection, security, discipl ne and religion. Because people need to know, and want to know, so many different things, the "how to" talk will always be in demand. The scope is tremendous, anything from, how to arrange the flowers to the best advantage, to how to prevent a nervous breakdown and other forms of mental illness. Ask yourself what you can do a little bit better than most people, and there you have your subject for a "how to" talk.

These three kinds of popular talks — the literary, the personal experience and the "how to" — by no means exhaust the possibilities of spellbinding addresses. Current affairs is another acceptable line. This may consist in a review of political matters at home and abroad, of the international armaments race, of racial problems, of the drug menace — the scope is literally worldwide.

A major problem for every speaker making a speech lasting anything up to an hour, without any v sual aids, is to maintain the audiences interest over that length of time. If you follow the hints given in Chapter 6 on this vital matter it might even be said of you what was said about Jean Jaurès, the French Socialist leader, when he discoursed on astronomy at a dinner party:

> "the walls of the room seemed to dissolve. We swam in the ether. The women forgot to powder their faces,

85

the men to smoke and the servants to go in search of their supper."

Chapter 10

THE ILLUSTRATED LECTURE

Its popularity — filmstrip, episcope and colour transparency — selecting the right pictures — variety — personal element — preparing the hall — talking about the picture on the screen.

THE modern illustrated lecture has a long and interesting ancestry. One programme of "Lectures for the People," dating back to Victorian times, tells of entertaining and educational sessions in the Drill Hall of a northern industrial town. Lectures on such diverse subjects as "Brain and Nerve, and their Work," "The Making and Unmaking of the Land", "Spiders", and "Magnets" and "Electric Currents," were delivered by experts on their subject, and illustrated by means of the oxy-hydrogen lantern, at a charge per person of 4d per lecture. In the days of our grandparents and great-grandparents, the "magic lantern," as it was called, with its brightly coloured glass slides, was a popular means of entertainment and education. The heavy, fragile glass slides and the cumbersome and sometimes uncomfortably hot "lanterns" have gone, superceded by more efficient means of projecting pictures. But the truth remains that when the eye reinforces the ear, the mind is able to retain more of what is told. Hence the importance of visual aids to the modern public speaker.

The old-fashioned "magic lantern" has given place to the cinema, or moving picture; the episcope, the film strip and the colour transparency. From the viewpoint of the public speaker the cinema film, whether you "shot" it yourself, or hired or purchased it, has certain disadvantages. You cannot keep stopping it to make sufficiently long explanatory comments as the scenes pass before the eyes of the audience. You can give an explanatory talk before or after, or maybe both before and after, the showing of the film. But it is better if the audience have the scenes of which you speak actually before their eyes at the time you tell them about it.

The episcope is a useful apparatus for small audiences. It reflects on to a screen, or wall, a highly magnified version of a picture in its actual colours. The picture may be in a book or on a postcard. This means that you can build up your own lecture from your own resources in the way of illustrations. You can hold each picture until you have told the audience all you want to tell them about it, or until you sense that they have seen and heard quite enough of that one.

The film strip, which requires its own special kind of projector, is another possibility. As the name suggests, this is a strip of film containing up to sixty pictures, or "frames." You can hire or buy film strips, or you can have your own strip made up from your own photographs. When you buy or hire a film strip a printed commentary is usually supplied with it. As with the episcope you can hold each picture until the audience has absorbed its meaning and significance.

But the most popular type of illustrated lecture is that making use of the colour transparency, often those taken by the lecturer himself. There is something peculiarly satisfying to the ego to display a pictorial record of your travels abroad to an admiring, and even slightly envious, audience! But, given by a novice, unaware of the many pitfalls that await the prospective lecture, such an experience can be a peculiarly boring one for the audience. They may be too polite to tell you what exactly they think about your collection of repetitive, some too light, some too dark slides, your halting and not always accurate commentary.

The older members will go away sighing for the good old days of "magic lantern" slides. You will be left wondering why you receive no more invitations to give your illustrated lecture on your holiday in the Tyrol or elsewhere. What a shame, after you had gone to all that trouble and expense!

Preparation for a successful illustrated lecture begins long before the appointed date. Buy a small notebook, and at the time when you take the photograph enter the place, the name and the date. This may save you embarrassment later, should you inadvertently, trusting to memory, inform your audience that this is a picture of the Jaffa Gate, Jerusalem, and someone calls out, "No, it isn't! That's the Damascus Gate! I stood there when General Allenby entered Jerusalem in 1917." Incidents like this can, and do, happen when speakers rely too much on unaided memory. As a further preventative of disconcerting incidents of this kind, it is a good idea to write brief particulars on the cardboard mount when you receive it from the processor. It is also good policy to mount the slides between glasses. This protects them from dust, finger-marks and scratches. It also keeps them flat during projection, as they are liable to pop out of focus when they are warmed up. To avoid accidentally projecting the slides sideways, or upside down, make a dot or other mark on the lower left-hand corner of the mount.

Reference has already been made to the boring type of lecture, with its seemingly endless succession of slides, mainly scenery and well-known buildings, the pictures varying in their quality from very light and faint to very dark, with details indistinguishable. If your slides are too light, or too dark, the purchase and use of a good light meter might make all the difference. There are plenty of photographic manuals on the market, to help you master the technical side, and maybe stricter attention to the booklet supplied with the camera is all that is necessary to enable you to correct the commoner faults.

Having assembled all your slides, the next step is to decide on your precise theme. What about that Italian holiday? According to the number of slides at your disposal you can decide whether to give a general talk on Italy and the Italians, or whether you will confine yourself to some specific area, say Rome, or Venice and the North, or whether you will concentrate on Italian beauty spots like the Isle of Capri, Naples and so forth. Having decided upon your theme, keep to it, and proceed to editing — strict and ruthless.

Reject all technically unsatisfactory slides, those out of focus, those over or under-exposed, those which are scratched or spotted.

Reject any near duplicates.

Reject anything and everything, however good, which does not really fit into the theme. These slides won't be wasted. They will fit perfectly into another lecture.

Reject those slides which only interest you, and you alone. After all this sorting out you may well find that you have an insufficient number of slides left to make a full evening's lecture, which can be anything up to an hour. A hundred slides is not too many for an hour's showing. But there is no necessity that all the slides should be of your own taking. In fact, for many lectures this would be quite an impossible requirement. If you propose to lecture on Rome, you would have no difficulty in taking your own photographs of the Colosseum, the Arch of Constantine, the Forum and the like. But what about the interior of, say, the Sistine Chapel? Perhaps you had a wonderful holiday in Bavaria, in the year of the world-famous Passion Play at Oberammergau. You would have no difficulty in photographing the streets of Oberammergau and the surrounding countryside. But to give the audience an idea of the Play itself you would need to buy the official set of slides, since photography is forbidden in the theatre during the performance. It is not only permissible and desirable, but it is sometimes essential to supplement the pictures of your own taking with bought ones.

The next step is to assemble the slides in proper order, bearing in mind that an illustrated lecture is like an un-illustrated lecture, in that it should be a coherent whole, with a recognisable beginning, middle and end. An airport picture of the plane that flew you to your destination, or of the ship in which you sailed, makes a good opening. For the middle section variety is the keynote. Mountains and fiords; parks and gardens, with close-ups of flowers and flower beds; quaint or historic buildings; and people, especially children, are the ingredients of a satisfying illus-trated lecture. In taking your pictures be constantly on the watch for differences between the British way of life, and the way of life in the country of your holiday choice. This could include subjects like men at work, perhaps showing the continental way of haymaking, or the Arab ploughing with an ancient donkey drawn implement that looks as though it had survived from Old Testament days. Children are a sure winner and holder of audience attention. One lecturer, in a series of slides depicting the Temple area in Jerusalem, included a picture of half a dozen Arab children, seated on a low wall, some of them sucking lollies. The relevant, but unexpected picture of this kind endears the lecturer to the audience, as well as maintaining the interest. Include those beautiful views you took, by all means, but never forget that people are also interested, perhaps even more, in people. Keep the human interest to the fore.

Watch for the unusual — the quaint old bridge or public clock, or street lamp, inn signs or murals painted on the sides of houses, shops or schools. If you find yourself in some beautiful park or garden, let at least one of your pictures be a close-up of a flower bed, and then listen to the "Ooh's" and "Ah's" of the delighted audience!

For this kind of picture you hold the camera above the flower bed. You photograph, not the stalks, but the glorious blaze of colour of the flower heads.

Read up plenty of background information to give your commentary an air of authority, and to enable you to answer any questions members of the audience may raise. If you are a beginner you would be advised to write out your commentary in full, to make clear in your own mind just what you propose to tell. Familiarise yourself with what you have written, and then reduce it to notes which you can take with you to the lecture room, until you feel you know your subject well enough to dispense even with them. It is painful to hear some novice announce, concerning the picture on the screen, "This is the Parthenon," or "This is the Corinth Canal," just that, followed by a pause, and then the next picture. Each picture needs to be supported by two or three carefully selected facts. When your picture of the Corinth Canal appears on the screen, you might say something like this:

"The Corinth Canal — a remarkable engineering feat. It's four miles long, cut through solid rock, and it shortens the voyage, from the Ionian Sea to the port of Athens by 202 miles. It took eleven years to construct, from 1882 to 1893. During the Second World War the Germans, before drawing out of Greece, blocked the Canal with a half-submerged merchant vessel."

The illustrated lecture is as demanding in its preparation as the unillustrated lecture. Magazine articles, guide books, travellers' memoirs, history books and encyclopaedias will give you the necessary interesting facts and general background information to make your commentary at once alive and informative. In addition to all this there is you — with your own particular slant and viewpoint, to give the proceedings some degree of originality and personality.

To round off the lecture, and to give it a satisfying ending, a photograph taken from the aeroplane, perhaps as it passed over the Alps on the homeward journey, or of the airport, or of the quayside from the boat that brought you back to England, or even of your own home to which you were glad to return — anything on these lines will make a happy ending to, we hope, a most interesting and informative lecture. It will also help if you commit to memory the opening and the closing sentences.

You are now ready to deliver your lecture. Your slides have been set in their right order, and right way up in their magazines. You have worked hard on your script, and are satisfied that each picture will be accompanied by brief, pithy, factual, relevant and occasionally humorous remarks. You would be wise to inspect the hall in which you are to deliver your lecture. Will it be properly blacked out? If not, your slides will not show to their full advantage. Is a screen and a projector to be provided? If so, is the screen the proper size and shape? Your own larger, square screen, may be superior to the small, rectangular one they suggest you use. Will your magazines fit the projector they would provide? Or would you prefer to use your own familiar projector? What of the electrical fittings? The wise lecturer provides himself with adaptors to fit any kind of projection plugs. He also takes with him a spare bulb. Whether you use your own screen and projector, or ones provided, take care to arrive at the hall in good time to see that the screen is up, and the projector is at the ready before the advertised time. If you are to act in the double capacity of lecturer and projectionist there is no necessity for you to stand beside the projector during the lecture. You can stand in front of the audience and manipulate the slides by remote control, with the aid of a device consisting of a cable and a switch, that is presuming you have an automatic projector.

If a friend acts as projectionist you will arrange a signal, perhaps a slight flash of a torch, when you wish to change the picture. This will save you saying over and over again, "May we have the next picture, please?" If you wish to indicate some detail of a picture you can use, either an ordinary pointer, or a handy little device the size of a torch, and using a torch battery, which projects an arrow head of light on the desired spot.

Until you know your commentary by heart you could keep your notes beside the projector, if you are acting as your own projectionist; or in your hand, or on the lectern, illuminating them as necessary with the aid of your torch if you are standing near the screen, in front of the audience. As the lecture proceeds, take care to talk about the picture on the screen, and about that picture only, and no other. This means you stop talking about it immediately it is replaced by another picture.

From the Victorian and Edwardian "magic lantern" lecture, to the Elizabethan colour transparency is a great step, and in the foreseeable future the illustrated lecture will retain its popularity — always subject to its being thoughtfully and carefully prepared and presented.

Chapter 11

THE SERMON

Its object — themes for today — preparation and construction — text — opening words — examples — quotations — conclusion — children's addresses — the greatest fault, and its remedy.

SUNDAY by Sunday, in thousands of churches of all denominations, sermons are preached by lay and ordained men and women. The decline in church attendance over the past several years confronts every preacher with the pertinent question, "Would the pews be better filled if the pulpits were better filled?" The modern preacher competes against powerful counter-attractions to public worship that our ancestors in the days of full Edwardian and Victorian churches never knew, notably the television and the motor car.

In some churches, when the vicar mounts the pulpit, the members of the congregation settle themselves as comfortably as they can in their hard pews, with resigned looks on their faces. For them sermon time is "Ten minutes when everybody goes to sleep," as the vicar makes a few trite and obvious remarks about the Gospel for the day.

Other preachers chat with their hearers, for up to twenty minutes, or so, in a pleasant, audible voice, throwing in a feeble joke or two, announcing a text, but never getting to grips with it, and really saying next to nothing that could possibly disturb anybody, nor brought any new enlightenment to a single soul, their simple hearers are sure to compliment them, saying how much they enjoyed "the little talk." Because he has given his hearers a pleasant twenty minutes this kind of preacher can delude himself that he is a success.

Higher up the scale we have the preacher who tells a familiar Bible story, but sheds no fresh light on its meaning, and makes no attempt to apply its teaching to everyday life in the 20th century. One such told the story of David and Goliath, and concluded with the trite remark, "There are many giants needing to be slain today," and left the matter there.

The reasons for the decline in church attendances are many and complex, and by no means are all of them the fault of the Church. Nevertheless some part of the blame lies with dull, unimaginative, irrelevant sermons offered to far too many longsuffering, and consequently shrinking, congregations. Happily this is not the whole truth. In any centre of population of any size there are sermons preached which really speak to the needs of the listeners.

What is the object of preaching sermons? It is to help people face reality. At first sight this does not seem to be a sufficiently pious or "churchy" answer to such a question, until we begin to reflect that "reality" is another word for "truth" and that there is a great deal about truth in the Bible. Christ said that He came into the world to bear witness to the truth. When the preacher does the same he is following in the footsteps of Christ. An effective sermon faces the hearer with the stark realities about himself, his strength and his weakness, the world in which he lives, and the supernatural forces ready to come to his help, if he is willing to receive them. Take any powerful sermon you have either heard, or read, and you will find that it fits into this definition of the object of preaching.

The first thing to bear in mind when you think of making a sermon is that a good sermon resembles a good speech on some secular subject, in that it should have a recognisable shape. It should be a progression, with an introduction, a middle section and a conclusion that summarises and challenges. The fact that you are talking about sacred matters is no excuse for inflicting upon your patient hearers a shapeless mass of loosely related platitudes and general exhortations to righteousness. Like any other form of public address a sermon needs a clearcut outline.

A sermon is usually based on a text from the Bible. This can be a single verse, or part of a verse, or several verses (e.g. a whole parable), or even a whole chapter. However short or long the text you choose, it should convey definite teaching, and sum up the sermon. A word of warning would not be misplaced here. Some sermons are irrelevant to the needs of the congregation because the preacher thought that he could make something of a certain text, but forgot to ask whether the resulting sermon would speak to the needs of that particular congregation.

Like any other form of public address a sermon needs an opening that grips at once the attention of the hearers. One good way to engage the interest of the congregation is to tell them just what sparked off this sermon in your mind. It may have been an incident you witnessed in the street, or a snatch of conversation on a bus, or a news item, or a question someone raised in conversation. This at once links what you are saying with everyday life. You can then explain anything that needs to be explained about the text, if there are any obscurities that call for comment. It is also useful to compare the rendering of the text in various versions of the Bible. The modern versions often have a way of sharpening up the meaning for modern hearers. The English language has developed since the days of James I and the Authorised Version. For instance "Take no thought for the morrow" does not, and never did mean, "Don't plan ahead." "Taking thought," in the days of James I, meant "worrying, being anxious." Modern versions bring out this change in meaning in the English

7

language. This kind of thing you will explain, if necessary, in your opening section.

The middle section of the sermon consists of such information as you have been able to collect about your theme. The Bible itself, Bible commentaries, church and general history, the lives of missionaries and other worthy people, the world of nature, your own personal experiences are some of the sources of information for you to draw upon. This will involve you in reading as widely as possible; and not only in reading, but in listening to the radio, and in viewing the television programmes as opportunity offers. We still meet preachers who boast that they never, or hardly ever, read a book. They tell us that they rely upon the Holy Spirit to fill their mouths. After listening to one of these preachers a thoughtful man remarked that he had never realised that the Holy Spirit could be so boring, so repetitive and so unoriginal! The way to inspiration in preparing sermons, as in preparing other kinds of public addresses, is through thorough preparation, drawing upon all possible sources of information.

The preacher's job is to proclaim the Gospel — the good news. He can only proclaim it successfully to the average hearer if he reinforces his proclamation with facts, reasons and explanations. People are no longer willing to accept the unsupported word of the preacher, even if what he says is undoubtably found in the pages of Holy Scripture. The preacher needs to demonstrate that what he says applies to life in the 20th century, as well as to life in Bible times. Hence the need for the preacher to keep abreast of what people are saying, thinking and doing today.

A real sermon contains sound teaching and instruction, as well as appeals and exhortations. A real sermon gives the generality of the congregation new facts, new and helpful insights into Bible truths, some new and helpful light on a perplexing problem, some specific new challenge to better living. This involves the selection of vivid instances, or "illustrations" as they are called, to fill that middle section. Carefully selected and apt illustrations make all the difference between a really soul stirring sermon, and one that is sound, but dull. But illustrations really must illustrate some point you are making. They must never be dragged in because they are so interesting. If you cannot find a use for that thrilling little anecdote in your present sermon, you will in a future one. Avoid the hackneyed old stories that congregations have been hearing for decades past. Another important point about illustrations is that they are the part of the sermon that people are most likely to remember, when your theories and exhortations have long since vanished from their minds. It is to be hoped that they also remember the truth the illustration illustrated? Be sparing in the use of quotations. If you read whole paragraphs, or more, from books, it may impress the congregation that you are a well read man, but the general effect is rather boring. Keep your quotations short and pithy, and relevant to everyday life. "Is Christianity your steering wheel, or just your spare wheel?" is more likely to be remembered by the average member of the congregation than a page or two from one of the poets or the classic prose writers.

When you have decided upon what facts you will use to fill your middle section, the next task is to arrange them in logical order, under two, three, but not more than four "heads," or divisions. This will help you to make that most desirable crystal clear presentation of your message to the congregation. Many a preacher has gained a reputation, among simpler listeners, for being "deep," because they could not follow his confused and confusing method of presentation. More discriminating listeners perceive that what passes with some for "depth of thought" is really

woolliness and muddiness of mind. Mud can give the illu-
sion of depth! Aim at being crystal clear, not clear as mud!
A study of the Gospels will convince that you can be clear
and deep, at one and the same time. So go all out for that
clear outline to your sermon.

The closing section of the sermon sums up and clinches
whatever you have been aiming to get across to your
hearers. Many listeners find that a brief summary of what
has gone before — a recapitulation of the main heads of the
middle section — helps them to retain more than they otherwise would. What has been said already in the chapter on
"The Parts of a Speech," concerning the conclusion of an
address, applies equally to the sermon, and need not be
repeated here. An apt quotation; a short, pointed story; a
challenge to choose one alternative or the other makes a
satisfying conclusion. If you follow this with a hymn
bearing on the same theme as the sermon, so much the
better.

What kind of themes should the preacher select in this
day of prestige symbols, keeping up with the Jones, the
rat race, the Welfare State and general material affluence?
The preacher is still needed because all these things do not
really cover man's deepest needs, nor satisfy his deepest
aspirations. Side by side with these features of national
life the nation's bill for tranquillisers, sleeping pills, intoxi-
cants, tobacco and escapist entertainment soars higher and
higher, in our vastly neurotic society. There is a great need
for preachers who can get beyond the symptoms to the
deeply rooted causes of man's ills. There is a need for
sermons on themes like these :

Why am I here? Is there a purpose, and if so what, in
life? Is there a life after death, or is this world all we can
expect?

Why do the good die young, good people contract
cancer, go blind, or lose a loved child or partner?

How can I "have faith," when the bottom seems to have fallen out of my world?

Does faith mean blind and unthinking acceptance of what preachers tell me I ought to believe?

Just what, if any, is the value of prayer?

How can I live peaceably with my sometimes exasperating husband/wife/children/relations/fellow members/workmates?

What about all those good people who seem to get along very nicely, ready to do anybody a good turn, yet who never darken the doors of a church?

Is there a God? If so, how can I be sure of Him, that He is interested in me, microscopic dot that I am against the immeasurable vastness of the universe?

It is getting to grips with practical problems like these, honestly facing up to the difficulties, that the modern preacher can serve the present age. For all his increased affluence and his better education, modern man still needs comfort and re-assurance, and a satisfying philosophy of life. Although we sometimes say that we know the difference between right and wrong, ethics and morals often raise questions of some complexity. If we cannot turn to the preacher for some guidance on all these subjects, to whom can we turn?

Sooner or later every preacher comes up against the question whether or not he should mention, or ignore, the great political issues of the day. A South African bishop, preaching in a Midlands town on the evils of apartheid, was himself denounced by some for bringing politics into the pulpit. The view that religion and politics should be kept strictly apart has had some notable supporters. One of them expressed himself thus, "Churchmen dabbling in politics should take note that their only task is to prepare for the world hereafter." That was Dr. Joseph Goebbels, head of the Nazi Ministry of Propaganda. He was rebuking those preachers who had had the courage and temerity to denounce the Nazi persecution of the Jews — a leading political issue of the day. The difficulty arises when political issues, as in this instance, and that of apartheid, are also moral issues. Matters of right and wrong are indubitably the preacher's business.

But since no political party has God in its pocket, so to speak, preachers should not ally themselves exclusively with any one political party. By all means let us keep party politics out of the pulpit! But an occasional sermon, like the South African bishop's on apartheid, reminds hearers that genuine Christianity has its feet firmly on the ground, even if its head is in the clouds! But there is a danger for the preacher who has had no firsthand experience of the problem of this kind. There may be some one, perhaps more than one, in his congregation, who knows far more about the problem than the preacher does, and on that account may have arrived at different conclusions to the preacher! An unrestricted diet of sermons on political issues would be a disaster for any congregation, but an occasional one, and passing references in sermons are in order — always provided that the preacher is really well informed about the matter on which he comments. Justification for this may be found in the pages of the Bible, notably in parts like the Book of the Prophet Amos, and in Our Lord's pronouncement on a leading political issue of the day, that of paying taxes to Caesar. So those who want to keep religion and politics apart should first get rid of the Bible — or else severely edit it!

A leading churchman recently pronounced denominationalism "as dead as mutton." Preachers will, therefore, refrain from wasting their own time, and the congregation's time, by denouncing the views and beliefs of other denominations. The enemy to be denounced is the secular spirit of the age, not the fellow believer who is working towards the same end as we are. There is a tremendous area of common ground in Christian beliefs, and preaching from this encourages our solidarity as Christians in face of common threats.

So far we have confined our attention to preaching to grown-ups. But what of the children and the adolescents in our congregations? The children's address in the morning service is not so much required as in former times. At a fixed point in the service children often leave for their own lessons in another part of the church premises. Nevertheless a brief talk to the children is still required in some churches. This also should be carefully prepared. "As I was coming along this morning I wondered what I should tell the boys and girls," or worse still, "I was sorry to see all you boys and girls here this morning, as I hadn't expected to have to give a children's address," are opening words that should never be heard. Bible stories, and stories from Church history, about heroes and heroines of the faith, make good material for children's talks. Or you can call in some visual aid, your watch or some other everyday object. Jesus often used everyday objects, flowers, hen and chickens, the plough, for instance, to illustrate spiritual truths. Providing you lead the children to some Bible truth about life you are in order to illustrate your talk with some commonplace visual aid. Keep exhortations—pi-jaw — to the minimum. A brief final sentence summarising the point you have tried to make, and then finish. If you go on to make a lengthy application of the moral of your talk, the children will not listen to you. It is not always possible to tell whether adults are listening, but by looking at them you can always tell when you no longer hold children's attention. One device for holding the attention right through the address is to ask occasional questions. To begin with a question is one way of securing immediate attention. As regards the adolescent — he or she will often remain for the whole of the service. An intelligent teenager is interested in those relevant themes already enumerated — if they are presented in a clear, orderly and interesting fashion. So, generally speaking, there is no need to prepare anything of a special nature just for that age group. Their I.Q. is as high as that of the average adult listener — in some cases higher!

The church is one of the few places where we can regularly talk to people about serious subjects, and challenge them to commitment. In spite of smaller numbers than in former days, is there any other subject which so regularly gathers together people for its consideration as religion? There is much encouragement to be found in these facts. There is also a challenge to exploit the opportunity to the utmost. Perhaps the greatest fault of the modern preacher is *Vagueness* — that pleasant amble to nowhere in particular and arriving there in about twenty minutes; that announcing of a text or theme, and never really getting to grips with it. Definiteness, not woolly sentiment, however pleasantly and amiably expressed, is the soul of the sermon. If the directions set forth in this chapter are followed this arch-enemy of effective preaching can be overcome, and the great opportunity offered to the preacher can be firmly grasped.

A preacher sees before him a mixed company of people. Financially and educationally they are generally better off than their forebears of a generation or two ago. But intellectuals and people who are comfortably off financially love and hate, are sometimes elated and sometimes depressed, sometimes worried, sometimes envious, sometimes tempted to do things unworthy of their profession, sometimes sad and sorrowful, sometimes sorely puzzled at the complexities of modern life, and at the way life has treated them.

The preacher's aim is to persuade them to think and

104

to act differently, or if they are already on the right track, to advance further along it, and to think and to act in that particular way more intensely. It is the preacher's privilege to be used to send puzzled people away enlightened, sad people away comforted, lukewarm people away enthusiastic, worried people away with new hope in their hearts, and all of them more strongly committed than they were before to the way of life set before us by Jesus Christ. Is the sermon an outdated form of communication? Not when the preacher knows his Bible, and how to relate its teachings, clearly and definitely, to modern life.

Chapter 12

RADIO AND TELEVISION

Opportunity for talks — how to submit — auditions — microphone technique — high standards demanded.

TELEVISION and radio are mass media on a scale never known before. In an ordinary public meeting you may, if you are fortunate, address an audience running into hundreds. If you speak on the radio, or on the television, your hearers might be reckoned in tens of thousands, even millions. National leaders have recognised the possibilities of these media for many years past. For good, or for evil, men like Franklin D. Roosevelt, with his fireside talks in the days of the New Deal; Adolph Hitler in his tirades against the enemies of Nazi Germany, and Winston Churchill in his stirring wartime speeches, influenced millions through the medium of the radio. Today Party Political Broadcasts are an accepted and regular feature of these media.

If you are ambitious to address the multitudes through the medium of either television or radio the first step is to listen and to view as much as possible, in order to inform yourself about the kind of material in demand. The B.B.C. needs a constant supply of talks by experts in their subject, and by people who have had some rather unusual personal experience they can describe for the benefit of listeners on the sound radio. If you are well versed in local history, or local customs, the people in your region may be interested. If music is your subject you might be able to give an informative talk during the interval in a concert. If your projected talk referred to a centenary, or other anniversary,

106

you would need to get your script into the hands of the B.B.C. at least three months before the event.

The biggest opportunity for radio talks is offered by the programme "Woman's Hour," which uses two thousand short talks every year. Men, as well as women, are given the opportunity to speak on this programme. The main stipulation is that the subject should be one of interest to women. If you are in any doubt about the interests of the contemporary woman, and indeed if you are not, listen to this programme regularly for a few weeks. Note the topics that come up. But a word of caution is called for here. You hear a talk on some subject in which you consider yourself, if not exactly an expert, very well versed — shall we say tatting?

"What a lot of interesting and helpful points were left out!", you exclaim, as though all that can be said about tatting can be said in five minutes or so. You set to work on a script describing other aspects of the fascinating art of tatting. It is a good script, full of interesting facts and helpful hints. You submit it, and to your surprise is it promptly returned. Once a subject has been used, that subject is "out" for months and months. Try again — but in a year's time.

The advent of local radio stations presents you with many more opportunities of being heard "over the air." Study their programmes. Listen to as many as possible, especially the magazine type of programme. Can you provide them with short items with a strong local slant, or about local personalities? You will probably be invited to broadcast your own script, or a member of the staff may interview you about your subject, and your tale comes over to the listening public in the form of question and answer. You will find the local radio station staff invariably courteous and helpful, doing all they can to put you at your ease if this is the first time you have broadcast.

107

If you have had some success in the difficult art of short story writing you might like to try your hand with the B.B.C. Listen to the stories they broadcast. Note the strong plots, the homely settings, and the twist at the end. There you have the recipe for stories that listeners like to hear. Note also how each story is timed to fit into its allotted slot, almost to the second. These stories are usually read by a member of the B.B.C. staff. But if you were successful in placing three or four stories with them, they might invite you to read your own tale "on the air." But first, they would obviously need to check on the kind of voice you possessed, of which, more later. But be well assured that the stories you submit must be of really first-rate quality, and they must be of the exact length required. Optimistic novices have been known to submit a batch of stories, already rejected as below publication standard, by various magazines, and of lengths varying from 1,000 to 5,000 words — and then been surprised at yet another swift rejection! Requirements change from time to time. Sometimes it is for the single story, and at others for a batch of five, or so, with a central character or situation. You will need to check in the "Radio Times".

In preparing your radio talk allow 120 words per minute. Remember also to allow for the introductory and the closing remarks by the announcer. On this basis a 15 minute talk would run to 1,800 words. Allow for the opening and closing announcements, and about 1,700 words would be right. Of course, some people speak more quickly when they are feeling nervous. The use of the tape recorder is invaluable here. Not only will it reveal elocutionary faults, but it will also enable you to attain the correct length for your talk. As you write your script keep your potential hearers in the foreground of your mind. Though their numbers may run into tens of thousands, do not make the mistake Mr. Gladstone made with Queen Victoria, and

address them as though they were a public meeting! You
will be talking to individuals, and to little groups of two,
three or four. Aim at chatting with them, rather than at
mob oratory! A touch of gentle, genial humour is always
helpful. But avoid the sick, slick, black kind of humour,
and anything merely vulgar and in bad taste. If you want
to tell a funny story, the most acceptable kind is one where
the joke was on you, the speaker. Nothing stiff and pompous is wanted. The tone of your talk needs to be kept
friendly and homely. This advice applies equally if you
aim to speak in the "Thought for the Day" programme.
People much prefer being talked to in a friendly manner,
as equals, to being preached at and lectured. You can be
authoritative without adopting an authoritarian tone of
voice and manner!

But before they give you the freedom of the air there
is the voice test. It would be cruelty to listeners to allow
anyone with an unduly high-pitched or gravelly voice, or
someone whose accent was so "broad" as to make their
talk incomprehensible, to inflict themselves on the public.
At the other extreme, you do not necessarily need a
course of elocution before you are fit to broadcast. If you
can read in reasonably clear and pleasant tones you will
pass the test, though it must be admitted that some fail,
unable to do justice to themselves, through sheer nervousness. For hints on how to overcome this weakness, turn
back to chapter 3. In this matter of voice production, as
well as in getting your talk into the exact shape and length
required, you will find the producer extremely understanding and helpful. He, or she, will not only point out your
elocutionary faults, but will also impart useful broadcasting
tips like avoiding touching the microphone when you turn
over the pages of your script.

Television offers relatively few opportunities for public
speaking. The local news programmes offer interviews rather

109

than straight talks. If you have written a book of local interest, or if you are a town councillor involved in some controversial issue about housing or immigrants or the like, you might be invited to an interview in the local television studio. Or you might find yourself confronted by someone who violently disagrees with your point of view on some question of public interest, and the two of you arguing it out on the little screen for five minutes or so. Viewers do not wish to be confronted with someone's face, however handsome or pretty, for any length of time. Even in Party Political Broadcasts the monotony of gazing at some political leader's face for minutes at a time is relieved by pictures of whatever he is talking about.

The religious programmes offer, as does the sound radio, a chance to preach at a Sunday morning service, or to take part in a discussion, as one of a panel of speakers. The coming of local radio stations means that many preachers will be heard "on the air" who otherwise would never have had the opportunity. But to return to television, your chances of being seen on the little screen on a Sunday morning, or of taking part in a discussion depends upon such factors as how well-known you are, and the part of the country in which you live. From Monday to Saturday religious talks are usually timed at just before, or just after midnight, when most people are in bed. If you feel it is worthwhile talking to a minimum audience, study these talks and submit your script to the television company concerned. The Churches' Television Centre, at Bushey, in Hertfordshire, has since 1959 provided training courses for ministers and others who are concerned to use television and radio techniques to get the Christian message across to the listening and viewing millions.

For full information about radio and television programme requirements, rates of payment, and addresses of the various radio and television stations, consult the section headed, "Broadcasting: Radio and Television," in the current issue of the "Writers' and Artists' Yearbook," in your local reference library.

To sum up; this is a difficult and specialised form of communication. Nothing but the best will suffice. Specific requirements are constantly changing, so that constant study, listening and watching is necessary. Its particular challenge and fascination lie in being able to reach such great numbers of people at one and the same time. Those who show signs of promise will find that B.B.C. and other officials will give them every assistance and encouragement.

PART III

PRESENTATION

Chapter 13

COMMON FAULTS

Vocal faults — choice of words — dialect — slang — clichés — archaisms — mannerisms — stance use and misuse of humour — length — critics can be a speaker's best friends.

ONE recipe for a good public speech is:

Firstly: *Get into your subject* — read it up as widely and thoroughly as you can, listen to all the experts you can, personally, or on the radio or television.

Secondly: *Get the subject into you* — right into your mind, so that you have all the facts readily at your command.

Thirdly: *Get the subject into your hearers,* by presenting it to them in such a way as enables them readily to grasp and absorb it.

The first two conditions have already been emphasized in the section headed "Preparation". The third condition is treated in this present section, "Presentation." With thorough preparation behind you your next task, without which all your preparation is in vain, is to communicate your facts and your message to the audience. You wish to persuade people who do not agree with you to accept your views. You want those who already agree with you to be confirmed in their opinions, and to act with a greater enthusiasm and intensity in whatever activity you are advocating. At the very least you want to give the people something they can understand, take away in their minds, and think over at their leisure. If you are to be successful in all this the right manner of presentation is vital.

You may have made such a long and thorough study

112

that you are regarded as an expect, and you proudly write the letters, "M.A.", or "Ph.D." behind your name. But it does not necessarily follow that you can communicate your knowledge to your hearers. We have known Masters of Arts and Doctors of Philosophy who have succeeded only in boring their hearers, and even in giving them a permanent distaste for the subject under consideration. You may feel absolutely convinced that you are right. But that is not enough. You then have to find ways and means of convincing the other fellow that you are right. Thorough preparation, vital though it is, is not enough. There must also be the right presentation of the facts and arguments, if the speech is to be effective. Aim at such a presentation of your case as will convince the deepest and shrewdest thinkers in your audience, and you will carry the rest with you. To fall into certain common faults can hamper, and even entirely prevent you from attaining the object of your speech. Certain faults concerning your choice of words will earn you a black mark with more discriminating members of the audience, which accordingly lessens your influence in that corner. Let us consider the main obstacles to an effective presentation of a speech.

All those laborious hours of preparation will be in vain if your voice lets you down. Attention has already been drawn to the major vocal faults, monotony and inaudibility. Those pearls of wisdom are wasted if the dullness of your delivery drives the audience to sleep, or if you adopt a conversational tone that travels no further than the front row. But as this problem has already been dealt with in the chapter about making the best of your voice, there is no further need to labour this point.

Your thoughts may be sound enough, but favourable reception by the audience is hampered if your choice of words in which you clothe them, is poor. Aim at simplicity, in words as well as in your sentences. Mastery of

113   8

the English language is not indicated by using the longest words you can think of, but rather in using just the right word, for that audience. Generally speaking, short, simple words like "try," rather than "endeavour" are to be preferred. Long, or outlandish words usually indicate a speaker who is trying to impress his audience with his learning, like the speaker who talked of "pulchritude," in preference to "beauty". Then there are horrible modern words like "containerisation" and "comprehensivisation," which the knowing speaker avoids. All subjects have their technical terms, and if you have to use them, do not fear to explain them if you feel that is necessary. Simplicity of speech also involves being direct in your expressions, for instance, saying "a lot", rather than "not a few". Choose words carefully, aiming at finding just the right one to express your thoughts, and adapt your words to that particular company. Avoid long, involved sentences.

Beware of words like "got" and "nice". "We have no bananas" is much smoother and less wordy than "We have got no bananas," or worse still, "We have not got any bananas." The word "got" is often superfluous, as well as giving an unnecessary ugly sound to the sentence, to those whose ears are sensitive to such faults.

"Nice" is an overworked word, and very often inappropriate to the matter in hand. "We thank our speaker for giving us such a nice talk," says the proposer of the vote of thanks. The speaker is anything but flattered or encouraged for he had aimed, not just to be nice to the company, but to rouse and stir them to action! Of course, "nice" is a fitting description for some talks and addresses. But speeches can also be informative, courageous, rousing, stirring, challenging, and to describe such an effort as merely "nice" depresses the speaker as well as the more discriminating members of the audience. Be careful with dialect words. Dialect is the speech of a particular region, and may not

114

be fully understood outside that region. The occasional use of dialect words is permissible if you know that the meaning will be understood. Slang needs also to be used sparingly, first being sure that it is up-to-date, since slang quickly "dates". A legitimate use of slang is in telling a story, when you are quoting what someone said. But slang should never be used for its own sake. Avoid even the milder swear words, and expressions like "O God!", which may mean something to some of the audience, if not to you. Avoid Latin tags and foreign expressions generally, unless you are quite sure that the audience can translate. You might, for instance, expect a meeting of businessmen to be familiar with the expression "Caveat emptor." Even then it would be advisable to give the translation. "Let the buyer beware," just in case the phrase was new to some. Sometimes the use of foreign words, place names, for instance, is unavoidable. Your standing as a speaker is not enhanced if, for example, you insist in pronouncing the last syllable of Oberammergau as "gaw" instead of "gow," as in "cow".

Another pitfall for the would-be public speaker is the use of clichés. These are outworn phrases, once novel, but the novelty has long since worn off. Beginners often use them unthinkingly. Here, for your guidance, is a list of some of the most familiar.

> In this day and age . . .
> It costs the earth . . .
> . . . just out of this world!
> Right, left and centre.
> When it comes to the crunch . . .

The cup that cheers, but does not inebriate.
> Drunk as a lord.
> Sober as a judge.
> . . . celebrating not wisely, but too well.
> . . . slept the sleep of the just.

115

. . . conspicuous by his absence.
. . . tear to shreds and tatters.
. . . and last, but not least.

These are some of the clichés in common use. You can probably think of a lot more, like "leave no stone upturned," "in a towering passion," "in the lap of the gods," etc., etc., etc. The constant use of them marks out the speaker as either too lazy to think up a phrase of his own, or else that his acquaintance with the English language was so slight that he did not realise that he was using a cliché.

Discriminating speakers also avoid archaic words and phrases like "Lo, and behold!", and "methinks." Instead of striving for effect by saying "peradventure," just say "perhaps," and "indeed," or "no doubt" rather than "forsooth."

Some words are quite good in themselves, but unless we are careful we find them intruding constantly, and the audience begins to count how many times we use them, instead of giving their full attention to our words of wisdom. Watch for such useful words as "definitely," "frankly," "actually," "candidly," "personally," "basically," "very," "extremely," and "quite." Used in strict moderation they are all good words, but a too constant use in one speech distracts the audience from the subject under consideration. The one letter word "I" also needs to be watched carefully. "I am of the opinion," "I would advise," "I consider," "I feel strongly," "I understand." To be a good public speaker involves learning the art of self-effacement. That constant "I," "I," "I" is a sure way of losing the sympathy and goodwill of an audience. Another trap is to address the audience as "you." Done too often it destroys the impression that you are "one of them." Make it "we," as often as you can, thereby identifying yourself with your hearers, and avoiding that fatal impression that you are a superior being, who is "talking down" to them. Although

116

you are the target of all eyes, your personality must not obtrude unduly. If it does the object of your speech will be diminished accordingly.

A nervous speaker will find himself pausing from time to time, and ejaculating, "Er . . . er," as he gropes for the next point. Providing you are aware of this natural frailty it will disappear as you gain more confidence. You may also find yourself repeating pet phrases from time to time, like, "See what I mean?", "O.K.?", or beginning too many sentences, "Well, . . ." Again, provided you have in some way been made aware of these words, it is not difficult to omit them.

Every speaker needs to know something about the use and the misuse of humour. A little genial touch of humour at the right time can relieve tension, when feelings seem to be building up towards an explosion. A touch of humour also relieves mental strain, and rests the minds of the hearers who are trying to take in a closely reasoned argument. Humour is also an aid to memory. A point dealt with and illustrated in a humorous way sinks more deeply into the mind. The last sentence underlines the necessity for the humour to be strictly relevant, and not just dragged in for the sake of a laugh. Humour should reinforce the point you are making. Kinds of humour to be avoided are sarcasm, cynicism, any form of sick or black humour, anything vulgar, blasphemous, in doubtful taste, or "chestnuts." If in doubt, leave it out. If the only funny story you know that would illustrate your point is a "chestnut," then be quite honest about it. Do not blandly tell is as though it was discovered today, when you know perfectly well that your grandparents, and maybe great-grandparents, were familiar with it. "This reminds me of that old chest-nut . . . ," is an honest approach if you feel that you really must tell a funny story at that point, but cannot think of an up-to-date one.

117

You may discover that humour is a very tricky business if you are speaking in a part of the country new to you. Dead silence may greet witticisms that brought roars of laughter elsewhere. The longed-for mirthful response may come unexpectedly, in a part of your talk you meant to be taken seriously. Beware of dialect jokes, if the dialect is not yours. As we indicated in the last chapter, the safest kind of joke is the joke told against yourself.

Keep your humour kindly, cordial and large-hearted. Keep it clean, so that every member of the family can listen without embarrassment. You can be funny without being "earthy." At all times bear in mind Lady Astor's technique for keeping the House of Commons in order, "Don't hit them on the head, but pull their legs."

Mannerisms, those annoying little habits and eccentricities that divert the audience's attention from your subject to you, are another problem. They take such forms as lolling and fidgetting, standing on one foot, putting both hands in pockets, rattling keys and coins, playing with your tie, putting on and taking off of spectacles, blinking, licking the lips, smoothing back the hair, consulting one's watch, scratching the head, pulling or stroking the nose, staring fixedly at the ceiling or at some point on the wall, leaning over the table and addressing the table top instead of the audience.

Fortunately mannerisms are not difficult to eradicate, especially in the early stages of your public speaking career, before you have had time to establish a habit. Once a kind and candid friend has made you aware of your little failing a little willpower is usually enough to dispose of the mannerism. When mannerisms persist for years it is usually because no one has made the speaker aware of his failing. The correct stance is another matter of importance, and it begins with your entrance. Some speakers slink in, head drooping, gaze fixed gloomily on the floor, as though this will be a great and trying ordeal for them, and perhaps for the audience too. Others have been known to strut pompously on to the platform, as though they were conferring a great favour upon their hearers, in graciously condescending to address them. Between these extremes comes the speaker who walks on to a platform as he might walk into the house of a friend, cheerfully and confidently. He glances round the audience, and even if there is only half the number present that he feels his address merits, he looks pleased to see those who have come to listen. When the chairman announces him, he stands up smartly, and faces the audience squarely. He stands easily and upright, firmly on both feet, which are slightly apart. Hands are a problem to the novice speaker. The experienced speaker is unaware of them most of the time. Some of the time they can be lightly clapsed either in front or behind. If the table is of the right height, the outstretched fingers may be in light contact with it. Or you can lightly take hold of the reading desk, or lectern — but don't clutch it hard or hang heavily on it! Hands on the lapels of the speaker's jacket gives a pompous effect, and hands in the trouser pockets may be a little too homely. From time to time change the position of the hands, smoothly and naturally not abruptly. As you become a more seasoned speaker you will find that your hands take care of themselves, and even make a few natural and spontaneous gestures from time to time.

In the matter of dress aim at neatness and attractiveness, but avoid ostentation. This rule applies to both sexes. Jangling bracelets, long strings of real or imitation pearls, gorgeous furs and stoles, and large hats with turned down brims, do not enhance the prospects of the female speaker. The important matter of self-effacement applies here. If the ladies present are wondering how much you paid for that fur coat, or whether that jewellery is genuine or not, they will not be giving their full attention to the weighty matters upon which you are addressing them. Neat and in good taste, neither showy nor slovenly, is the rule of dress for both sexes.

One of the commonest of all faults among public speakers is that of talking for too long. Keeping your eye on the clock is a golden rule. Always try to find out your time limit before you begin to speak, and stick strictly to that limit. If you can find out the required length before you even begin to prepare your speech, so much the better. You can then try out your talk for length with the aid of a tape recorder. This is very important, for many a man has first been talked into a better frame of mind, and then talked out of it by an unimaginative speaker with no sense of time. Sometimes the speaker goes on and on because he has never realised that no audience wants to know all there is to know about a subject. If there are other aspects they want to know about, the opportunity to ask will arise in question time — if the speaker has left enough time for questions! A speaker who has thoroughly re-searched his subject will have far more material than he can pack into one talk or lecture. He must then make a judicious selection of the facts he feels would most interest that particular audience. To try to cram everything he knows about the subject into one talk is fatal. He may only succeed in giving his hearers mental indigestion. On the other hand, the speaker who finds that he has not enough facts to enable him to fill in his allotted time may find he is repeating himself — and you have to be an exception-ally fine orator to hold the attention of your audience if you start going over the same ground in almost the same words. Audiences rarely grumble if the speaker finishes short of his allotted time, though you can rely on a dis-gruntled few to complain that they have not had their money's worth. But only in exceptional circumstances will an audience forgive the speaker who seriously over-runs his time limit. Some speakers have been known to complain that it is a pity that people are unwilling to sit for an hour, or even less, listening to an address on a serious subject, whereas they will sit for three hours in the cinema, watching some frivolous film. But if the film was as boring as some addresses and sermons, and if the cinema seats were as hard as some in our halls and churches, people would not sit in cinemas either.

The alert speaker discerns the signs of boredom, and he finishes his talk as quickly as possible. Signs of unrest are all too plain to escape the notice of the speakers whose eyes are on his audience rather than upon his manuscript.

People here and there with closed eyes. Perhaps they find they can listen better that way — or have you made them feel drowsy? That man has consulted his watch three times, and the last time he held it to his ear. Yawns, coughing, shuffling of feet and people moving to the exit, these are all ominous signs, well in evidence when the speaker carries on beyond his time. It sometimes happens that a speaker finds it impossible to get "on the same wave-length" as his hearers. Then there is no satisfaction to any one if he grimly plods on to an increasingly restive audience, until he has said all that he has come prepared to say. Close in as quick and dignified a manner as you can, is the best course on such a melancholy occasion.

Sometimes it is necessary to lengthen a speech at short notice, perhaps because another speaker has failed to put in an appearance. Here the well prepared speaker will draw upon the surplus of information he accumulated during his period of preparation. He will go into more detail, or he will quote two, instead of one, instances of the points he wishes to make. If, for some reason, the meeting starts late, and a shorter talk is required, he will reverse the process, and streamline his talk, omitting details and one

121

or two instances.

To win favour with your audience — keep your eye on the clock, close while they could still take more, and learn to stop talking just before they stop listening!

Glancing back over this list of the more common faults prevalent among public speakers suggests the importance of the kindly, constructive critic if we are to develop in the art of speaking effectively to an audience. The critic can help us to overcome so many faults that mar our effectiveness. No criticism, no progress, is a maxim applying to public speaking as much as to many other human activities. A critic can be a speaker's best friend — if the speaker will listen. Even in those shallowest of criticisms, deriving from ignorance wedded to illwill and envy, there is a golden grain of truth — if we are not too proud to recognise it. If the criticism is unduly harsh, it is wise to take the truth from it, and forget the harshness. What hope of progress is there if we resent being told that we stray from the point, go on too long, are above the heads of a good proportion of our hearers, tell stale jokes, or mumble indistinctly as though we had a mouthful of plums? Many a good public speaker can point to the growing points in his career as times when a candid wife, or other well disposed and knowledgeable person, hurt his pride by telling him of faults like these.

You can, of course, be your own critic. One way of learning to do this is to listen to other speakers. Without being censorious, consider their methods and presentation of their talks. Was his talk of the right length? Was all he said relevant to his subject, and suited to his audience? Did he emphasize the key parts? Was all the information he gave really accurate? Did he quote actual instances to make clear his points? Was there a clearly discernable outline to his talk? Did he explain any technical terms with which some members of the audience might be unfamiliar?

Was he audible at all times, or did he sometimes drop his voice at the end of sentences? Had he any distracting or annoying mannerisms? Ask questions like these, and realise why that particular speech was so well received, and why this one was almost a fiasco. Then apply what you have learned to your own efforts. Nor must we forget the mechanical critic — the tape recorder, which we cannot accuse of unfair bias or envy!

Most speakers who fail to make the grade do so because no one ever told them of their defects and failings, and they never learned how to detect their own shortcomings. Or it may be that they were told, but either grew discouraged and gave up speaking in public, or else suspected the motives or competence of the critic. It is encouraging to know that so many of our speaking faults can be eradicated once we are made aware of them. After all this it would be a pity if you then fell into the error many people fall into about faults, that is of acting as though admitting a fault means there is no need to correct it! "I know I go on at length, but I keep on doing it, I just seem to get carried away with my subject." What a pity if, after spending so much time getting into your subject, more time in getting your subject into you, that for the want of a little self-discipline and willpower you fail to get your subject into your hearers!

123

Chapter 14

THE USE OF NOTES

Shall I read it? — Memorise it? — or use notes? — how
copious? — layout — specimens.

On a visit to London you have perhaps included a session
in the House of Commons, listening to a debate. If you
have never had the privilege, perhaps you have seen Parliamentary debates depicted on the cinema or television screen.
Did you notice something? The Members of Parliament
did *not* read their speeches. In fact the rules of the two
Houses of Parliament expressly forbid the reading of
speeches, except by Ministers of the Crown, and by the
Leader of the Opposition, when making considered state-
ments at the dispatch box. This is a very sensible rule.
Reading a speech inevitably robs it of spontaneity and
naturalness. The speaker is out of touch with his audience.
His eyes being fixed to his manuscript he cannot follow
audience reactions, and detect those signs of restlessness
and loss of interest indicated in the last chapter. There is
no intimate feeling that the speaker is talking to each
member of the audience personally, which is one of the
marks of good speaking. In short a read speech tends to be
a dull speech, and dullness is a cardinal sin in a speaker.
Think of those occasions where people meet to listen to
someone "read a paper." They are hardly numbered among
the liveliest of gatherings!

Readers who have already formed the bad habit of
taking a full manuscript on to the platform, or into the
pulpit, and reading it word for word, will perhaps be

protesting that there are solid advantages to a read speech. The possibility of forgetting anything is obviated. The audience gets the benefit of every word of those beautifully rounded sentences you have taken such pains to shape, not to mention those flashes of wit of which you fear they may be deprived if you relied entirely upon your memory. All this is true, but, as we shall see, there is a more excellent way to ensure that these benefits are passed on to the audience.

Other speakers have been known to dispense entirely with a manuscript, made a stupendous mental effort to memorise what they have to say, and then recited it to their audience. You need an exceptionally good memory to make a success of this method. It was employed, with great success, by certain Victorian lecturers. But as they grew older they found their minds apt to "go blank" in the middle of their oratory. If you are a good actor, accustomed to committing long passages to memory, you might succeed in declaiming your speech with dramatic effect, without a breakdown. Even then you would be wise to enlist the aid of a prompter, just in case your memory failed.

The real answer to this particular problem is to train yourself to speak from adequate notes. Just what "adequate" means will vary from speaker to speaker, and you will have to find your own level. In spite of what has been written about a full manuscript, it is a wise move to write out your speech in full — always provided that you do not take it with you on to the platform. When you read over what you have written it is at once plain whether you have produced a jumbled mass of more or less related ideas and facts, or whether there is a clearly defined outline, with a clear progression of thought from a clear beginning to an equally clear ending. Writing out in full clears the thinking, as well as shapes the ideas. When you

125

have written all you can, go over the script and cross out all you can, as you visualise the audience and their needs and capacities. Having revised and re-written your script, until it presents a logical sequence of ideas, your next task is to reduce it to notes which will accompany you to the place where you will speak, and guide and sustain you as you address your hearers.

If you are at all doubtful about your ability to speak from fairly brief notes, consider this undoubted fact. In private life the average man and woman has the ability to find suitable words to clothe his, or her, ideas and express himself, or herself, quite clearly. If this is so in private life, why not in public life? The ability is still there. Neither nervousness nor self-consciousness can dispose of this innate ability, and ways and means of disposing of these enemies of the public speaker have already been indicated. If you have something you know to be worthwhile to say, something you believe in, are deeply interested in, and know quite a lot about, the words will come. Suppose that you are living in rented rooms. You hear of a house for sale at a price you think you could just about afford. But before you can proceed to action you must first persuade your wife, when you get home. You do not write out several sheets of foolscap, setting forth your financial position in great detail, together with a full, closely reasoned statement of the facts for and against the suggested purchase, and then read the whole screed out to her! You may set down a few figures on a scrap of paper, and present the case for purchase from that. The words and phrases in which you clothed your ideas would vary according to the state of your education, as would your arrangement of your ideas. You are confident that you have a sound case to present — and you find that the words come.

Notes are essentially memory joggers. Clear, adequate, well laid out notes remove undue strain on the memory, and that haunting fear that you might forget, and stand there like a dumb fool in front of your audience, your mind a ghastly blank, amid a pitying and highly embarrassed silence. Experienced speakers are not ashamed that they take notes with them to their appointments, though this fact may be by no means obvious to the audience. On one occasion one of the finest orators of our time, with a slightly misplaced gesture, sent his sheet of notes flying into the audience. Thanking the man who returned them, he said, "Perhaps I shan't need them, but it's just as well to have them." Here is wisdom, for distracting, disconcerting things can happen in a public meeting, things that interrupt the flow of the speaker's thoughts, as well as taking away the attention of the audience. Some one faints or has a fit, some one tramps noisily in or out, someone has a prolonged fit of coughing or sneezing, or even falls asleep and snores loudly, or someone is summoned from the audience perhaps because of some domestic emergency. Possession of clear, well laid out notes reminds you, and the audience, just where you were when the emergency arose. If you feel it necessary you can recapitulate, and then make a new and clear start. Under normal circumstances notes will also prevent you from overlooking some important section of your talk.

Notes should be kept to the minimum amount to enable you, at your stage of progress in the art of public speaking, to present your case effectively. Too many notes can obtrude between speaker and audience. For that reason never take a wad of notes on to the platform. If you do so you can rely on some members of the audience counting the number of times you turn over to the next of the seemingly endless succession of sheets in your hand, or on the table or reading desk, when they ought to have been giving their individual attention to the weighty theme you are expounding for their benefit. At the other extreme, if

127

your notes are too brief, and this is the first time you have attempted this talk, you may show a disturbing tendency to wander from the point, having lost the thread of the argument. You may find yourself "waffling" on to an increasingly bored and restless company. Finding the happy medium between too many and too few notes depends upon the degree of your experience of public speaking, and upon your familiarity with, and the depth of your knowledge of your subject. You will find that, when you have delivered a certain address a number of times, you can give it independently of notes. Even so it is just as well to have them with you, in case the unexpected happens, and your thoughts and the thoughts of the audience, are temporarily scattered.

Beware of the idea that to be able to dispense with notes on all occasions is a desirable prestige symbol. We have all heard admiring comments about the speaker who "never needs a note." As the words come tripping so easily from his tongue, some are wondering how often he has given that talk before. Or it may be that an analysis of the talk reveals little more than a few broken remarks on some subject, spoken in a pleasant, facile manner. However strong the desire to become in great demand as a speaker, and to sun yourself in the warm admiration of large audiences, please note that there is neither disgrace nor discredit in using notes, and in letting the audiences see that you use notes. When you rise to speak, make no attempt to hide your notes. Just lay them openly and unostentatiously, on the table, lectern or reading desk.

Do not scribble your notes. Either type them, or write them in block letters, clearly visible at 3 ft. from your eyes. Emphasize the main headings by underlining them. Clearly written, or typed, notes remove any need to stoop when you consult them from time to time. Write out any quotations in full, or you may run the risk of some knowing person

128

putting you right on the *exact* wording when questions and discussion time comes. The same hint applies to any essential statistics you need to support your argument. A well drawn up set of notes is a summary of your talk, and gives you the general trend, without the exact wording of the original script. Though you may not use the exact words of the original you will find that, as you grow in experience, just as good words, or even better, come readily into your mind as you stand there before your hearers. You will be encouraged, too, as you find how much information can be typed on to one side of a piece of paper measuring 8 ins. by 5 ins. This is a very handy size for talks lasting up to half an hour, or even more. As you mature, or when you have given that particular talk a number of times, you may find that you can manage very well with what notes can be written on one side of a postcard. There is no set rule about the amount of notes a speaker should take with him, or her. As indicated earlier in the chapter, each one must find his own level, and just how much, or how little, prompting you need to keep you thinking fluently while on your feet. In Chapter 9 we considered three kinds of popular talks, the literary, the experience, and the "how to." Let us draw up a sheet of notes for each kind of talk, beginning with the literary kind, in this instance say, H. G. Wells.

Perhaps a television serialisation of one of his novels gives you a topical peg upon which to hang your talk. You decide that you will try to present a general picture of his life and achievements, rather than concentrating upon any one facet of his life and activities. You gather your material. You set it in order. You write out your projected talk in full. Then you set about reducing this mass of information into concentrated form. If you do not feel too sure of yourself, and you wish to avoid a fumbling, hesitating start, you could write out the opening sentence in full. It might

9

read something like this:

"Many of you are following the adventures of Mr. Lewisham (or Mr. Polly or Kipps or whoever is being currently portrayed) on the little screen."

You could continue your introductions by asking what kind of man was the creator of these characters. If you are old enough to have listened to him broadcasting, you could add that he spoke in a rapid, high-pitched, almost squeaky voice. This may evoke similar memories from old members of the audience. You have connected your subject with the lives of your hearers, and secured their favourable attention, for the time being at least. After that you could recount the main events of his life in chronological order, working in your own comments and explanations. Any essential dates (not more than three or four), and other facts to create a framework would appear in your notes, together with any brief quotations, either from his writings, or what people said or thought about him. The last sentence is as important as the first sentence, determining the impression you leave with your listeners, always providing that you have managed to keep them listening for so long, of course! In this instance you might conclude thus:

"He set out with such high hopes, but he died a bitterly disappointed man — for mankind had refused to be prodded along what he thought was their road of salvation." Along these lines the notes for a talk lasting twenty, thirty, forty or more minutes, according to the time limit imposed, would look something like this.

H. G. WELLS

Many of you have been recently following the adventures of Mr. Lewisham on the little screen. What kind of man created such characters?

EARLY POVERTY

Herbert George Wells, born 21/8/1866, at Bromley,

Kent. Son of shopkeeper and domestic servant. Apprenticed to draper at Hythe. Pupil teacher at 18. Science degree at London University. Determined to escape from poverty. If he could, so could others. Key to understanding his life. Science plus education.

HOPE FOR MANKIND

Scientific romances, "Time Machine," "First Men in Moon," "War of Worlds," "World Set Free."

Social novels about "meek, mild, obstinate, little common men." "Lewisham," "Kipps," "Polly." "Air of good-humoured sympathy." 1st World War. "Mr. Britling sees it through." "God the Invisible King."

DISILLUSIONMENT WITH MANKIND

Post-war social problems. "Outline of History," "Shape of Things to Come." 2nd World War completes disillusionment. Died 13/8/1945.

Defective (over-optimistic) view of human nature. Mankind refused to act like Mr. Polly and escape environment. "He set out with such high hopes, but he died a bitterly disappointed man — for mankind refused to be prodded along what he thought was their road of salvation.

Such a set of notes would enable you to lengthen or to shorten the talk as circumstances demanded. In order to lengthen it you could include more details about his poverty-stricken boyhood, and include more particulars about the books he wrote. To shorten the talk, simply reverse this process.

Perhaps you are attracted towards the "experience" talk. You have a job that brings you into constant contact with people. This is obviously the kind of work people like to hear about, rather than a description of industrial or chemical process, where the human element is very much in the background. Let us suppose that you are a clergyman. You might draw up a set of notes on lines like these.

A PARSON'S LIFE

There is a quaint idea that a parson has a very soft job
—preaches twice on Sunday and then takes the rest of
the week off. This is almost the exact opposite of truth.
VARIETY is keynote of parson's work. Three kinds.

ADMINISTRATIVE

Business side—letters, formfilling (and signing), reports,
committees, preside over business meetings, councils.

WORSHIP, PREACHING, TEACHING

Services, Sunday and weekday. Speak at weekday meetings, men and women. Confirmation classes. Training
classes. Requires preparation — reading, radio, TV.

"Parson does not stand up and turn on the talk like
turning on a tap." Must first store mind with information.

PASTORAL

Getting among the people. Visitation of sick and aged.
Christenings, weddings, funerals. Youth work.

Interviewing people with problems. Chaplaincies —
hospital, prison, industrial.

Optional extras — talk to Rotary, Soroptimists, Women's
Institutes, Townswomen's Guild, Darby and Joan,
schools. Work one day a week? Seven if you're not
careful!

Do you feel drawn to the "how to" kind of talk? Perhaps
you have been asked to address the Young Wives, or the
Parent-Teacher Association. They would certainly be interested in some information on how to bring up their children
as good citizens. So you draw on your experience, and talk
to them on lines which can be summarised thus:

BRINGING UP JOHN AND MARY

Many parents have a secret fear that their children will
develop into juvenile delinquents. They have such tantrums, they tell lies, they steal.

Children — primitive little creatures, born self-centred

132

and with disposition to flout law, if they can get away with it. Give them 4 gifts.

AFFECTION

Must be shown. Physical contact. Time to play with, listen to, advise if requested. Give them yourself, not just what money can buy. Affection promotes.

SECURITY

Insecurity prime cause of delinquency. Settled pattern of life. Parents in harmony with each other. Unfair to ask child choose when inexperienced.

DISCIPLINE

Moderation! Firm, definite, kindly, same yesterday, today and tomorrow. To smack or not to smack?

RELIGION

Coming to terms with supernatural. Prayers. Bible stories. Prime importance of example. Parents display Christian virtues.

Given all four, overwhelming probability they'll turn out well — a credit to you, and a comfort to you in your old age!

To sum up: first write out your talk in full, and then reduce it to the minimum of notes required to jog your memory. You may need to experiment to decide just how many, or how few, notes you need to give you a sense of security as you stand before your audience. Go over your talk, at least once, in private, using your notes only, before you mount the platform. Leave the full script at home, trusting in the average person's innate ability to clothe clear ideas and strong convictions in suitable words. Never be ashamed of needing notes, and never try to hide them from the audience. Having spent some time and mental effort on drawing up suitable notes, resist any temptation to wander away from them, to explore some attractive side-track.

STICK TO YOUR NOTES is a golden rule, if you would avoid delivering a wandering, waffling kind of speech. The purpose of having notes with you is not only to save undue strain on the memory, but also to help you to keep strictly to the subject under discussion. The exceptional speaker may make a brilliant speech without the aid of notes. But for the average speaker it is a choice of a good, to-the-point speech with notes, or an inferior, wandering speech, perhaps with an important section omitted, without notes.

Chapter 15

QUESTION TIME

Best part of the meeting — audiences are reasonable — average
questioner eager to learn — chairman's duty — educating the
audience — long, involved questions — the hostile questioner —
patient, courteous, reasonable — silly questions — cranks —
crying babies — 7 hints — when no questions come.

In time past people were often more content to sit back,
and to accept, without question, all the learned speaker
told them. But the modern speaker is usually asked to finish
his address in time to allow members of the audience to
put their questions to him. Just how much you enjoy
question time will depend upon how well you know your
subject, and upon how equable is your disposition. Question time is necessary because you cannot deal exhaustively
with every aspect of your subject. Neither can you be expected to foresee every single point upon which individual
members of the audience may crave enlightenment. But providing you know a lot more than you put into your talk,
and provided you can keep calm, courteous and goodhumoured under possible provocation, you need not fear
question time. In fact, you may look forward to it as the
most fruitful and enjoyable part of the meeting, the time
when the issue is really clinched.

Audiences, in the main, are very reasonable. They do
not expect their speakers to be either infallible or omniscient.
A slip of the tongue, or an occasional error of fact simply
shows that the speaker is human, and therefore as prone
to error as they are. Do not be unduly depressed if you
are caught out in some minor error. Inadvertently you
refer to the "1817" instead of the "1812" Overture. "Yes,
of course! How stupid of me!" you smile, when someone

puts you right. The audience smiles with you, and thinks none the worse of you, perhaps even better, because of your goodhumoured acceptance of correction.

Generally speaking, the larger the audience, the slower they are to begin asking questions. In the more intimate atmosphere of the smaller meeting people feel freer more quickly to express their doubts, and to confess the gaps in their knowledge. An abundance of relevant questions is a compliment to the speaker. At least it shows that they have listened to you!

The average questioner is eager to learn more, and this is your opportunity to help him. He may question you on some aspect of the subject you felt you could not include if you were to finish within the set time. Or it may be some angle you forgot to include. He may ask for fuller factual information upon some point, or ask you to make yourself clearer on another point. He may challenge some statistics you quoted, or the validity of some conclusions you drew. Straightforward questions like these can often be answered by quoting some of the facts you have in reserve. It might be, for instance, that your statistics are more up-to-date than his — at least we'll hope so! No one knows everything there is to be known about any subject. So, from time to time, without any feeling of shame or guilt, you can answer, "I don't know." If you feel inclined, you could appeal to the audience. "Does any one here know?"

The question may be a stupid one, revealing that the questioner has hardly started to think about the subject. But however stupid you think the question, and the questioner, you must not say so. To you it may seem that the answer is so glaringly obvious that it is a waste of the audience's time to put it. You may be strongly tempted to say, "Good heavens! Can't you see that? It's as plain as a pikestaff,!" and so hold up to public ridicule a quite sincere, though rather mentally dull man or woman. The

136

audience will like you the better if you make some such
reply as, "I remember that point worried me too, at one
time," and then go on to explain, as simply as possible, the
fallacy behind the difficulty.

A good chairman can be of great assistance to a speaker
at question time. A man stands up, and instead of putting
a short, pointed question, proceeds to make a short speech,
interspersed with several queries. An efficient chairman
would call him to order, and remind him that this is the
time for questions, not speeches. But what if the chairman
fails in his duty, and allows this fellow to ramble on?
What is your best course? We sometimes see speakers, in
such circumstances, furiously trying to scribble down the
main points upon which enlightenment is requested. Others
refrain from writing, and strain their memories trying to
retain each point raised, and in the correct order. If the
chairman lets you down there is a better course than either
of the two mentioned. Take the questioner gently to task.
"That's really a speech you made! Supposing every questioner did that! And you've not been content to ask just
one question, like the others. However, let's sort out the
points you raise. Now, would *you* mind, for the sake of
clarity, putting your points to me, one by one, and I'll try
to answer them." Watch your tone of voice as you talk to
him. Keep it light and goodhumoured rather than heavy
and severe. Then the onus is on him. Even if you cannot
answer the questions he raises, at least you will have taught
him a little about good manners in a public meeting. It
is not good manners to "hog" the time, when others also
have their questions to pose. Audiences sometimes need
educating in the rules of procedure at meetings, as well as
speakers and chairmen!

Sometimes a member of the audience will not quite make
a speech, but will ask a long, involved question which
leaves you wondering just exactly what reply he wants.

137

The chances are that, if you are puzzled about what precisely the questioner wants to know, the audience is equally mystified. Put on a puzzled, but anxious to help expression, and say, "I'm afraid I don't quite follow. Could you possibly simplify what you've said?" The onus is then on him to explain just exactly what it is he wants to know. After all, the audience expects you, the speaker, to make your meaning crystal clear, to them; so why should they not return the compliment to you? At such a time, provided you retain your goodhumour, you will find that you have the sympathy of the audience.

Occasionally, if you are burdened with a weak or inefficient chairman, you may find that you have to restrain some one who asks so many questions that others are deprived of their opportunity to do so. If he is so thirsty for further knowledge you can always invite him to talk to you after the meeting.

The examples cited above are all instances of questioners who, though sometimes a little muddled in their approach, in the main entertain feelings of goodwill towards the speaker. But there are times, few and far between, when you may encounter a hostile questioner. His hostility may arise from a feeling of personal antipathy towards you, who may have upset him at some time. Or you may have, quite unintentionally, trodden upon one of his pet prejudices during the course of your address. Or he may quite honestly have arrived at the opposite conclusions to you about the subject under discussion. On the other hand his opposition may have no connection either with you personally, or your subject. He may have come to the meeting, having walked out of his house immediately after a blazing row with his wife! Or he may nurse a grievance against life in general, because he has not made the social or financial progress he thought he ought to have done, with his abilities. He is looking around for someone he

138

can "take it out of," and you happen to be at hand! He deliberately sets out to prove you wrong. He brings in personalities, and makes snide allegations against your motives and character. He may use dishonest devices, like quoting a few words you undoubtedly said, but quoting them quite out of context. He may even be quite rude. Such characters are fortunately in very short supply, but they do turn up at meetings now and again, and it is well to know how to deal with them.

The worst response is to lose your temper, and reply in kind, in loud and heated tones. If you feel your temper rising as he makes his sly allegations, ask yourself why he is behaving like that. Happy people do not behave thus. The late Lord Milner, asking how he could be so patient with a certain obnoxious and irritating character, replied, "The man's miserable, and misery has no manners." You ask yourself which of the causes cited above is making this man miserable. Thinking along those lines you find your anger subsiding, and a sense of pity taking its place. Agree with him, as indeed you would with any questioner, as far as you can. In soothing tones, in direct contrast perhaps to his, say something like, "I'm glad you raised that point. Lots of people find difficulty there," or "It's a good thing to have the other point of view brought out so plainly." The audience is immediately with you, and in case of need may even come to your help! The great thing is not to meet aggression with aggression. Be practical, and meet unprovoked attack with patience, courtesy and sweet reasonableness. Perhaps he asks you to reply with a straight "Yes" or "No" to his question, implying that to fail to do so is to be guilty of evasion. In many instances this may well be true. But you may need to point out to him that there are times when such a reply is impossible, perhaps quoting the classic instance of this kind of enquiry, "Have you stopped beating your wife?" If he would be so kind

139

as to re-phrase this question. . . . Patience, courtesy and sweet reasonableness need be no indication of softness on your part, but rather a civilised form of firmness that raises your standing with the audience. They will appreciate a fair and reasonable answer, whether your hostile questioner chooses to do so, or not.

Then there is the would-be comedian, who deliberately asks a silly question, and sets the audience laughing. Laugh along with them, however weak the joke, and then reply, "Come, now! Do let's be serious." During the actual course of your speech a heckler may interject more or less serious questions from time to time. They may take the form of a short sentence, or just a single word, like "Why?" The chairman's duty is to restrain such, perhaps by a gesture, and a severe look and shake of the head in the interrupter's direction. This will not interfere with the flow of your words. You can ignore the heckler, in the hope that this will discourage him from further interruptions. Or you can take the matter in hand at once. "All in good time, my friend! I'll answer questions when I've finished — and not until." If he persists after this, either the audience will tell him to keep quiet, or else he should be asked to leave.

There are times when it is good tactics to toss a question back at a questioner, where his question is based on, to you, an obvious fallacy. A shrewd question will reveal the fallacy to him, and to the audience, and at the same time obviate any need for a more or less prolonged explanation. You are also helping the questioner to provide his own answer, by thinking out the matter himself. Sometimes you get, not so much a question as a dogmatic statement, contradicting you. "Well, *I* think . . . ," or "It's *my* opinion that . . . ," he begins. In such an instance ask him, "Why?"

Then there is the crank, the man with the one track mind, a pet view that he seriously overworks. Take care not to get involved in a long and complicated public

140

argument with him. Be courteous, but firm. As often as not his question is not strictly relevant, which provides you with a good reason for asking for the next question. He may put his question in some such form as, "What is your opinion of. . . ?" If your opinion can be stated in a few words, state it. If he seems disposed to enter into a long controversy, try to be diplomatic. "This is a big, a very big, subject you've raised. I really don't think we could do justice to it at this hour, in the time at our disposal. So perhaps we'd better not try to deal with it now. Next question, please." At least you have not evaded the question; you have given your opinion as asked, and the demands of courtesy have been observed.

To hostile questioners, hecklers and cranks we might add another trial to public speakers — the crying baby. You have just got into your stride, when the noise begins. The mother succeeds in soothing and silencing the little mite. But only for a minute or two, and then there is another outcry. At this juncture the chairman, or a steward may do their duty, and the interrupter is removed. But just suppose that neither chairman nor steward does anything about it. Privately you may be thinking that parents really ought to have more sense than to bring a baby to a public meeting, especially an evening one. The little dear ought to have been snugly tucked up in his cot hours ago. But no indication of your annoyance should reach the audience. You stop speaking. You smile sympathetically and apologetically in the direction of the noisy infant, and say, "I really can't compete, so would you mind. . .?" A sympathetic murmur goes over the audience. The mother carries out the interrupter, and you resume to an audience still smiling pleasantly over this human little incident. But any show of irritation and annoyance on the speaker's part, and down he goes in the estimation of the audience. His prospect of influencing the audience to his views deteriorates accordingly.

Another form of interruption may take the form of the shuffling of feet, the rustling of papers or persistent coughing, either while you are trying to answer their questions or during your actual speech. Try to ignore it, but if the noise really becomes intolerable, stop talking, look severely in the direction of the noise, and then resume with a slight change of tone. If that does not work, appeal to the chairman to do his duty.

Here are seven hints on how to be happy during question time:

1. Know a lot more about your subject than you put into your speech.
2. Try to put each questioner in a good humour by agreeing with him as far as possible. "You certainly have a sound point there, but. . . ."
3. Be direct, avoid evasiveness, and as often as possible answer with a plain "Yes" or "No," backed by your reasons. If you don't know, say so.
4. Be patient, even with stupid and involved questions. The points raised may seem relatively unimportant to you, but not to the questioner.
5. Be brief, but not abrupt.
6. Be courteous at all time, even under provocation from some rude oaf. Never descend to his level.
7. Keep your temper — nobody else wants it!

Follow these rules and you will keep on good terms with your audience though the subject discussed is a highly controversial one, arousing strong feelings both for and against.

Occasionally, when the chairman asks for questions, none are forthcoming. But do not despair for this may be due to any one of several reasons. The audience is not accustomed to being given this opportunity, or they are too shy or too dull to respond. Or it may be that you have covered

142

your subject so thoroughly that nothing remains to be asked! This is highly unlikely. It is more likely that you have gone on at such length that the audience is thoroughly tired of the whole business, and wants either to go home, or else get on to the customary cup of tea and gossip with which their meeting ends.

Chapter 16

PORTRAIT OF A SUCCESSFUL SPEAKER

Worthwhile — Demosthenes and George VI — importance of
words — importance of character — sincere, conscientious,
friendly — friendliness means cheerful, patient, imaginative —
stockpiling ideas — how books help — entertain, inform,
influence — formula for success.

So you still want to be a public speaker, even after reading
about the amount of preparation demanded, and the
various pitfalls and trials that await you? But a moment's
thought brings it home to us that no really worthwhile
task is easy. Think of the concert pianist, for instance.
Behind his public recital lies years of hard practice, before
he gains the mastery of the keyboard that enables him to
bring deep and satisfying pleasure to his hearers. So it is
with the public speaker who has really mastered his art.
The long hours spent in thorough preparation enable the
public speaker to bring pleasure, and often much more than
pleasure, to his hearers.

It is probable that you, who read this, possess a normal
speaking voice, free from any marked impediment. If so,
you have a big start on some who, in spite of an original
handicap, still contrived to make good as speakers. One
classic example is that of Demosthenes, the Greek orator,
who lived in the 4th century B.C. He was afflicted with a
painful stammer. In order to cure this defect it is said that
he adopted the extraordinary device of practising speaking
with his mouth full of pebbles! In order to accustom himself to the noisy audiences of the day he practised speaking
on the seashore, making his voice heard above the roar of
the breakers.

In our own time we have had the encouraging example

of the late King George VI. He was afflicted with a pain-ful speech impediment. Yet one of the most moving of all radio talks came from his lips, his 1939 Christmas broad-cast, when he quoted the poem, "The Gate of the Year."

In that period of the "phoney war" he brought new courage and reassurance to the uneasy and apprehensive millions, on the threshold of the fateful year, 1940. Behind that most effective talk lay years of hard and courageous struggling to overcome his speech defect. If men with initial difficulties like these could make good, the prospects are so much the brighter for those of us already equipped with normal voices. Nervousness, correct intonation of the voice, collecting the right material in the right quantities, probing questioners and other problems combine to remind us that Bunyan was right when he saw the Hill Difficulty in the path of someone going somewhere worthwhile. How-ever, as someone else has said, don't stand looking at your hill—climb it!

So you want to be a *speaker!* Surely there are enough talkers about already! We need more men and women of action, rather than more talkers! It is not more words we need, but more deeds! Words, mere words, are not what is most needed today, but action! It is true that some-times we speak disparingly of "mere words," though we would never think of speaking of "mere dynamite." For words can be even more powerful than dynamite, as a glance at man's long and chequered history will show. Many of the deeds we so much admire would never have been performed if the right words had not first been spoken to galvanise the performer into action. Words, the speaker's stock-in-trade, can bring encouragement to the depressed, and enlightenment to the ignorant. They can inspire to the wrong, as well as to the right kind of deeds. For better or for worse, words are power, for good or for evil. For twentieth century examples of the power of words in the mouths of orators we can cite Churchill, Roosevelt and Hitler. Mere words, indeed! Mere dynamite!

The fact of the matter is that the public speaker is participating in one of the most important activities of our time, or of any other time—the communication of ideas. Words are his vehicle to that end. Before we can have the desired action, the right idea, clothed in the right words, must first be communicated to those we wish to influence. With the development of the great mass media—the radio, television, cinema and the popular press—the speaker does not play the important part he once did. But in spite of the availability of the mass media a reference back to Chapter I will demonstrate that the public speaker is still in demand. He brings a personal touch to the matter of the communication of ideas impossible to the mass media. If you disagree with something said on the radio or television, or with something printed in a newspaper, you can answer back, and in due course, if you are lucky, you may get a satisfactory response to your comment, query or request for fuller information. With the public speaker the response is immediate, and if you are still not quite clear, you can there and then press for a fully satisfactory reply. The radio and television may bring better speakers than you and I will ever be, right to our firesides. But the herd instinct has not yet died out of human nature, and people still like to meet and to mix together, listen to a good speaker and discuss matters with him after he has finished his address. In this business of the communication of ideas public speaking is a well tried and proved method, and there are no signs that it will die out in the foreseeable future.

The first fifteen chapters of this book have stressed the importance of ability—ability to make the whole audience hear, ability to find the right facts for that audience, ability to present those facts in an acceptable way, ability to answer questions honestly and succinctly. But, for maximum effectiveness, the ability to do all these things is not enough. Behind ability must lie a certain kind of character. The absence of certain character traits soon make themselves obvious to any thoughtful audience, and the speaker's influence upon them is diminished accordingly.

Sincerity is the very first quality an audience demands. Do you really believe in what you are trying to persuade them to do? Do you practise it yourself? Any suspicion of talking with your tongue in your cheek conveys itself at once to the audience, and is fatal to whatever it is you are advocating. Sometimes, when an audience has suffered under some immature speaker, a kindly member will say, "Well, at least, he was sincere." The sincerity shone through the inaudibility, the muddied thinking and arrangement of facts. There is hope for the sincere speaker, for he has the foundation quality to commend him to any audience. Without sincerity the wooing voice, the logical arrangement of facts and arguments are all in vain, as far as the thinking, discriminating part of the audience is concerned. You can, of course, fool some of the people all the time, but the test of any speech is its effect upon the thinker and the honest enquirer. You will find him very hard indeed to convince, if you yourself are not absolutely sincere in what you advocate. The matter of motives comes into this as well, something we touched upon in Chapter 1. Refer to it again. Mixed motives are common to all speakers. But if the predominant motive is a sincere desire to serve your hearers, you have a firm foundation upon which to erect the superstructure of your speech, talk, address, lecture or sermon.

Conscientousness, or thoroughness, if you prefer that word, is another indispensible quality in the speaker. It shows itself in many ways. No amount of learning and ability to charm your audiences will compensate for its absence. It shows itself during your preparation, in assembling more information than you will need for that particular talk, so that you are well prepared for any questions that may be put on matters not covered in the address. It shows itself in your taking time and trouble to dig out lesser known facts, and to present unusual angles on your subject. It is demonstrated in the way you prepare the notes for your speech, clearly written or typed, and in just sufficient quantity to see you through. The conscientious speaker, too, arrives in good time at the meeting place, so that any necessary consultations with the chairman, or other officials, can be held in an unhurried manner. Conscientiousness may be a pedestrian virtue, but it certainly makes for the smooth running of a meeting.

A third desirable, indeed essential quality in a speaker, one which covers a very wide field, is that of friendliness. The audience warms instinctively to the speaker with a friendy bearing. Reference has already been made to its importance, in the advice on the best way to make your entrance, "walk on to the platform as you would into the house of a friend." Think of the qualities we like to see in our friends. We like them to be cheerful. Dismal Desmond is never in demand as a companion! So the speaker should look cheerful, even though he may be feeling distinctly apprehensive, even fearful, as he notes the presence in the audience of various intellectuals. Looking cheerful does not mean that you must wear a silly grin on your face all through the evening. Smile, by all means, from time to time, as occasion demands. For the rest of the time contrive to look pleasant, thugh serious. Whether you are a man or a woman, never forget that the most important thing you wear is the expression on your face. This is especially important when you sit up on a platform, the target of all eyes. As you make your speech, be sure that the cheerfulness is reflected in your tone of voice. The fact that you are actually looking cheerful will almost automatically

148

guarantee this.

We like our friends to be patient with us when we do or say something stupid, or when we show our ignorance. Audiences like speakers to display that kind of attitude too, to their shortcomings. The effect of a good speech can be ruined by a display of irritability, or bad temper. Patience with an interruptor, voluntary or involuntary, or with a hostile or stupid questioner, greatly enhances the speaker's effect upon his hearers. Some of them may be thinking, "If I were up there, I'd be strongly tempted to give him an answer he'd never forget! I'd feel very much like showing him up for what he is!" Then you respond with a plain, direct and courteous reply, and at once your stock rises with the audience. The courteous, but firm, reply to some obstreperous individual is never wasted on the audience, and in the long run, not usually upon the difficult one. We find it easier to be patient with the defects and infirmities of others if we remind ourselves that we also have our faults and failings, which others must endure. As Thomas à Kempis reminded us, if you cannot make yourself such a one as you would, how can you expect to have others in all things just to your liking?

Imagination, the ability to put yourself in the other fellow's place, and feel as he feels, is another mark of friendliness. Our feelings towards some one who bores and wearies us with his much speaking are usually anything but friendly! That is how the audience feels towards the speaker who has never cultivated a sense of time, and who is blind and deaf towards the signs of unrest in the audience as he maunders on and on. A lack of sensitivity to the feelings of others can spoil even a well prepared and soundly constructed speech, when the speaker is oblivious to the time factor. There are people who are longing to ask questions, and at the rate you are going on you will leave no time for that profitable and enjoyable part of the session. A friendly smile may play continually across your features, as you deliver your speech, but to disregard the time factor is discourteous, inconsiderate, and the reverse of friendly conduct towards the audience.

The flexible and mellifluous voice, the Master of Arts or the Doctor of Philosophy degree are wonderful assets, but they are greatly offset unless they are backed by the right kind of character and personality, summed up in the words SINCERE, CONSCIENTIOUS, FRIENDLY.

The man and woman with average ability, plus these personality traits, will be far more effective than the polished elocutionist and brilliant intellectual who is lacking in them.

Another important matter demanding attention in this final chapter is that of stockpiling the ideas we encounter, and which may be of use to us in time to come. Some form of storage system is needed, so that we can refer quickly to those statistics, or to exactly what someone said or wrote. One way is to collect cuttings from magazines and newspapers, and to file them in envelopes, under their appropriate headings. If the information you wish to preserve is in a book, you could type out the facts on a piece of paper, and file it with the cuttings. Another way is to buy a thick exercise book. Copy into it the information you wish to store. Leave a margin at the left-hand side of the page, and enter into it the title of the item. Number the pages, and make an index at the back of the book of all the items collected. Another useful habit is to carry a small notebook around with you, and jot down in it any ideas that may occur, which may be of future use in your talks; or any items of information you may pick up when you are, perhaps, browsing in the local library, and particularly the reference section, for the acquisition of necessary information. Standard works of reference, like the many volumed Encyclopaedia Britannica, and that mine of useful information in one volume, Whitaker's Almanack, are available at all reference libraries. If you are really baffled about where to turn for the information you require, do not be afraid to enlist the aid of the librarian. If the book containing the information you seek is not on the library shelves, he will know from whence to obtain it. You will, no doubt, build up your own small library of books bearing on your chosen subject, or subjects. This will save you from perhaps inconvenient visits to the public library when facts are required, or checking of facts is necessary.

The way to become a good tennis player is to play tennis. The way to become a good writer is to write. The way to become a good gardener is to work in the garden. Therefore the way to become a good public speaker is to speak in public. This is the truth, but not the whole truth. We also need guidance, expert and authoritative, if we are to make the success of these activities we ought to make, and could make. But experts and authorities, in human form, are not always at hand. Hence the necessity for informative, authoritative books. Without guidance we can go on making the same old mistakes, year after year, until they become fixed habits. As the late Stanley Unwin, the publisher, remarked, "There are few things that books cannot help us to do better." How many gardeners, for instance, who have never thought it worthwhile to read a book on the subject, make elementary mistakes like burning all their garden rubbish, when a good proportion of it could be turned into compost to ensure bigger crops next year? Or they never prune their gooseberry bushes, and would not know how to set about the job, in any case. Many an amateur gardener would reap much larger crops, if he could only be persuaded to read a few suitable books. So it is with public speaking.

It is sad to encounter the speaker who goes on making the elementary mistake of addressing the people in the front two rows, instead of aiming at the people in the back row. No one has ever told him. He might be offended. But a book could challenge him on this elementary, but vital point, about the right use of his voice. Mention has been made of gardeners who seem never to have heard of the necessity of pruning. We meet speakers, too, who would be more effective and in demand, if they learned to prune their addresses, and to keep them within the prescribed time limit. There are men who pride themselves on their long record of "taking the chair," who have never learned the elementary truths that a chairman stands towards the speaker in the same relation as a host towards his guest, that a chairman should always be seen very definitely to take second place to the speaker; and that a chairman's remarks, or address, should never exceed ten minutes, and is appreciated even more if it is kept within a five minute limit. These are some of the common faults a speaker's friends sometimes hesitate to tell him about. A Christmas or birthday present of a suitable book, "I know you're an old hand at this, but you may pick up a hint or two," or "Now you've taken up speaking in public you may find this helpful, old chap," could lead to a marked improvement.

It is the privilege of the public speaker to entertain, inform and influence people. At its best public speaking can do all three at the same time. Admittedly some subjects lend themselves to the entertainment angle more than others. The point is to beware of, and to avoid, the heavy and ponderous approach. Set out deliberately to avoid imposing any quite unnecessary mental strain on the audience, if you wish to keep them with you for the duration. There is nothing wrong in their enjoying a speech on a serious subject. The good humour in which such an approach puts them makes them the more ready to receive information, and to be influenced in the direction you wish them to be. On the other hand, there are times when an audience needs to be made to feel thoroughly uncomfortable and dissatisfied with themselves, rather than to be amused. These varying situations are a challenge to the public speaker, a reminder that no worthwhile job is an easy one. The art of making advice agreeable has never been an easy one!

Success as a public speaker means that you attain your object, whether that be to entertain, to inform or to influence, or maybe all three. In a nutshell success depends upon your realisation that:—

What you say is important—therefore you must spare no pains in gathering and selecting the right material.

How you say it is more important still—the tone and audibility of your voice, the orderly and logical presentation of facts and arguments.

What you are matters even more than what you say and how you say it. Character and personality are all-important. To sincerity, conscientiousness and friendliness we may add humility, the willingness to admit mistakes, and to learn from them.

Successful public speaking adds up to the right things, said in the right way, by the right kind of person. Proceed along the guidelines laid down in this book, and with patience and pertinacity, you will find that all three conditions are within your attainment.

INDEX

154